HEALTH
CARE-TOONS

HEALTH
CARE-TOONS

HEALTH CARTOONS
BY

ED FISCHER

WELLNESS QUEST CHALLENGES
BY

JEFF HAEBIG, Ph.D.

WELLNESS
QUEST™ BOOKS

ROCHESTER, MINNESOTA

NOTICE TO READERS

This book offers numerous ways to enhance well-being; we hope you find great pleasure using its ideas. The book is not offered as medical advice or as a guide to diagnosis or treatment of any disorder. If you suspect that you have a medical problem, seek competent medical care.

ACKNOWLEDGEMENTS

Special thanks to artist Greg Wimmer for designing the cover; Ben Mahle for his editing work; Steve Lansing of Lifespan Associates, Rochester, MN for typesetting, book design, and encouragement; Bev and Carl Bartness of Modern Printers, Faribault, MN for their caring attitude in printing Health Care-toons; and to the many health professionals in Rochester and around the United States and Canada who provided ideas for this book. The authors also express gratitude to Extra Newspaper Features for allowing the reproduction of certain cartoons for this book.

For information please write Wellness Quest Books, 1541 7 1/2 Avenue N. E., Rochester, Minnesota 55906

ISBN 0-9623600-0-7

Library of Congress Catalog Card Number: 91-91068

First Printing, July 1989
Revised Edition, July 1990
Revised Edition, July 1991

Dedication

This book is dedicated
to

Ed Fischer's mom
Helen
and Jeff Haebig's parents
Bob and Fritzi

and to all parents who
teach health and happiness
through good example.

T A B L E   O F   C O N T E N T S

GETTING IN SHAPE FOR HEALTH WITH CARE-TOONS: THE WINNING EDGE

Donald B. Ardell

The heaviness of burdens crushes us, we sink beneath it, it pins us to the ground... the absence of a burden causes man to be lighter than air, to soar into the heights, take leave of earth and his earthly being...

Milan Kundera
The Unbearable Lightness of Being

Most athletes would do more than extra training to improve their jump shots, or shave seconds from their swim, bike, and run times. They would eat, sleep, think, talk -- even mate differently from "normal" people if doing so would offer an elusive edge toward a gold rather than a silver medal. Similarly, "ordinary" folks want to "lighten their burdens," whether these be excess weight, stress, or obligations. But whether you are an athlete or an "ordinary folk," you can have more "success" in your life, by adding humor, fun and joy to your daily experiences.

Through reading this book, you can make humor and play a part of your daily workouts, as if you were a world-class athlete of life. Lightness will be a major element in your daily training regimen. Unlike hard sessions at ball sports, swimming, biking, or running, you can't overdo happiness. This form of interval training will give you the truest edge.

Lightness workouts will protect the hard-driving "life athlete" from burnout. Lightness attitudes and practices will help you overcome illness and speed recovery from injury. Lightness interval work will increase productivity and morale. And, lightness can be contagious: Your buddies, family members and associates might soon lose weightiness just being around you.

This fun book will show that lightness is not only cartoons, jokes, and horsing around, but encompasses applause, approval, and exaltation as well. Lightness embraces caring, support, and joy, and thrives in positive, cheerful settings where everyone feels special. This book will guide you into such settings and offer you the chance to both lighten your load and add to your lightness of being.

Donald B. Ardell, Ph.D., wrote the landmark book High Level Wellness: An Alternative to Doctors, Drugs and Disease. He also wrote seven other wellness books including Die Healthy, and Wellness: The Body, Mind and Spirit, his two latest. He is the publisher of the somewhat outrageous quarterly newsletter entitled the ARDELL WELLNESS REPORT. Readers can obtain a copy by sending a self-addressed, stamped ($0.45) envelope to ARDELL WELLNESS REPORT, 9901 Lake Georgia Drive, Orlando, FL 32817.

INTRODUCTION

An overview of health concerns
and how this book can help out.

ED FISCHER

Boldly examine the ways you choose
to think, feel and respond to life.

SEEK THE TREASURE WITHIN!

THEN PASS ALONG THE RICHES!

ED FISCHER

HEALTH CONCERN: The majority of diseases and deaths today result from poor lifestyle habits. Strong feelings of self-worth move people to reduce these health risks, and seek higher levels of well-being.

THIS BOOK will examine simple things that can be done daily to expand self-worth, and promote health and happiness more fully.

HEALTH CONCERN: There are vast numbers of environmental health risks today. More than ever, people need to choose products wisely and be conscious of threats to their safety.

THIS BOOK shows simple ways to use self-care and safety practices to reduce health risks and avoid accidents that will protect and prolong life.

HEALTH CONCERN: Countless health problems result from too much soft living and unwise eating.

THIS BOOK explores how to eat and exercise wisely to build total fitness and feel more energetic and alert.

HEALTH CONCERN: Feeling closer to people improves both physical and mental well-being. Studies show that people tend to live longer when they feel a connection with others.

THIS BOOK offers easy-going wellness challenges that can help people expand social skills and feel closer to others.

HEALTH CONCERN: Healthy living requires that people take control of their lives without controlling others.

THIS BOOK highlights ways to take greater control over one's thoughts, feelings, and behavior while remaining playful.

HEALTH CONCERN: Tobacco is the "number one" preventable cause of death and disability in our society.

THIS BOOK examines tobacco health risks along with ideas for reducing or eliminating those dangers.

HEALTH CONCERN: Misuse and abuse of alcohol and drugs creates havoc and destroys lives.

THIS BOOK defines drug and alcohol problems, and suggests ways of managing them.

HEALTH CONCERN: Feelings have a powerful impact on health. They can heal people, or tear them apart.

THIS BOOK shows how to improve one's mastery over emotions to overcome ill-tempered feelings, expand happiness, and improve relationships.

ED FISCHER

HEALTH CONCERN: Difficulties are a part of life. Conflict and illness can result when these problems are not skillfully handled.

THIS BOOK identifies problems which pull people down and prevent them from moving ahead in full stride. Solutions are offered to help people glide through life more joyously.

HEALTH CONCERN: Failure to work together to preserve human and natural resources will produce grave results.

THIS BOOK encourages people to uplift their spirit and help others each day with small, loving acts that enrich and extend life.

HEALTH CARE-TOONS
USER'S GUIDE

1. Skim through the book, enjoy the care-toons and consider how each "Wellness Quest" challenge relates to your life. Complete a new challenge each day. Choose those challenges which extend and enrich your life; experience the zest and joy which results!

2. After performing a variety of daily "Wellness Quest" challenges, select one to perform for seven days. Record each day's success on the "Score Card" found on the next page.

3. If you want to form (or break) a "mild" habit, continue to perform the same wellness challenge for two additional weeks, (21 days total). To form (or break) a "strong" habit, perform the same wellness challenge for three more weeks, (42 days total).

4. Invite your family and friends to join the wellness activities. Ongoing health and happiness is enhanced when wholesome living is supported by others close to us.

CONGRATULATIONS for stretching your health potential; enjoy the countless physical, mental, social and spiritual rewards!

SPECIAL NOTE: This book is intended to inspire healthful living. The information is meant to complement the advice and guidance of health care professionals, not replace it. Just to be safe, discuss any major change in your diet or activity level with your doctor before starting, especially if you're over 40, have a medical condition, or are out of shape.

To ensure ongoing success, extend your efforts beyond these pages and seek additional health information and medical advice when necessary. Enjoy your Wellness Quest!

Recycle this book!
Share it with your family and special friends!

WELLNESS QUEST SCORE CARD

NAME: _____ DATE: _____

WELLNESS QUEST ACTIVITY I PLAN TO PRACTICE: _____

_____

WHEN, WHERE, AND HOW I WILL GO ABOUT THIS:_____

_____

HEALTH BENEFITS I PLAN TO RECEIVE:_____

_____

DIRECTIONS: Each day you complete your Wellness Quest activity, record the date of your success in the boxes below.

FIRST SEVEN DAYS TO VICTORY!

14 MORE DAYS TO FORM OR BREAK A MILD HABIT!

21 MORE DAYS TO FORM OR BREAK A STRONG HABIT!

EATING
CONCERNS

Launch a sensible eating program which won't come crashing down. Develop sound habits that will guarantee ideal body weight and tip-top fitness for many good years!

ED FISCHER

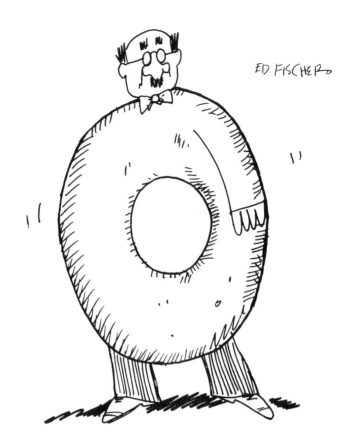

ED FISCHER

YOU ARE WHAT YOU EAT

Foods greatly affect moods, bulge bellies, and broaden backsides. To look your best, eat 2 daily servings of low-fat dairy foods; 2 servings of meat, poultry, fish or meat alternative such as dried beans or peanut butter; 4 servings of fruits or vegetables; 4 servings of enriched, fortified, or whole-grain breads and cereals.

Write down the food groups listed above. Each time you eat today, record one point under the group(s) that each food belongs to. At the end of the day, see if your diet is balanced and complete.

EXTENDED CHALLENGE - *Plan "balanced meals" for the entire week. Write down what you'll eat for breakfast, lunch, and supper - then stick to it. If necessary, plan wholesome snacks.*

ED FISCHER

SUGARY SNACKS CAN DISH UP A
FULL COURSE OF MENTAL FATIGUE

Sugar and other added sweeteners can cause a rapid rise and fall of blood sugar levels. One common result is a sudden burst of energy followed by drowsiness. Smart snacking can help prevent this from happening. Overweight people are advised to skip snacks altogether.

Replace sweet snacks today with low-sugar, whole-grain snacks, plain popcorn, crispy vegetables, fresh fruits, and juices without sweeteners. Notice how much more energetic and alert you feel.

EXTENDED CHALLENGE - *Use DOS (Do Other Snacks) for two weeks. Observe your energy as you replace sweet snacks with those suggested above.*

ED FISCHER

WE'RE GOING AFTER THAT CHOLESTEROL BUILD-UP

Plumbers can't unclog your plugged up blood vessels. To help prevent heart disease, strokes, and other vascular problems, work to keep your arteries clean. Eat fewer foods with saturated palm and coconut oils, chicken and beef fat, cocoa fat, lard, and butter.

To lower saturated fat, eat baked or broiled chicken or fish without skin; limit red meat to four ounces or less per serving; avoid foods with palm and coconut oils; use margarine instead of butter.

EXTENDED CHALLENGE - *Participate in a cholesterol test. If your score is high, consult with a health care professional trained in nutrition and physical fitness. Higher scores may require further evaluation and medical attention to help bring it down. Changes in diet or exercise are especially important to help wash out excessive cholesterol and protect against further pileup.*

ED FISCHER

COOKIE JAR JUNKIES LOSE THEIR HEADS

If cookie and candy cravings drive you crazy, decide whether you're hooked on sugar, or are simply a cookie compulsive. Next decide whether you care to break free from your sugar slavery and replace the high calorie sweets with more wholesome treats.

Avoid grocery shopping on an empty stomach to resist buying sweets; use a grocery list and stick to it. Having problem foods around is begging for trouble even when you vow to eat only a little.

EXTENDED CHALLENGE - *Once cookies and other sweets are cleared from the house, buy only smaller servings on special occasions.*

EXPERTS SAY DRINK EIGHT GLASSES OF FLUID A DAY, BUT NOT ALL AT BEDTIME!

Water cleanses body cells, aids digestion, promotes regularity, and helps prevent kidney stones, urinary tract infections and hemorrhoids. Drinking fluids also aids chapped lips, colds, flu, fever, heat exhaustion, gas, diarrhea, and food poisoning.

Start with one glass of high-quality drinking water when waking up each morning; continue with one between meals, and before retiring each evening. To refresh your body, drink natural water that is low in sodium, or better yet, without sodium.

EXTENDED CHALLENGE - *Build your intake of fluids to 6-8 glasses a day. Water, herbal tea, and fresh fruit juices without sugar or sweeteners are excellent choices.*

READ WHAT YOU'RE EATING

Read the key ingredients on the foods you buy. They're listed in order of weight and provide an excellent clue as to what you're eating. Notice whether sweeteners, fats, and salt are among the first five ingredients mentioned. If so, a different brand might prove healthier.

See which foods have the lowest sodium, sweeteners, and percentage of fat, determined by dividing total calories per serving by nine times the grams of fat; 90 calories divided by (5 grams of fat times 9) = 50% fat.

EXTENDED CHALLENGE - *Using the formula above, hunt for foods containing 30 percent fat or less. For a 100 calorie serving, two or three grams of unsaturated fat are acceptable. Limit yourself to one serving so as not to exceed your limit.*

ED FISCHER

IS YOUR EATING OUT OF CONTROL?

Eating disorders include obesity, anorexia (dieting to the point of starvation), and bulimia (overeating followed by self-induced vomiting, fasting, or using laxatives to get rid of the food). Many life-threatening medical problems can result, such as heart failure and gum disease.

If you suspect an eating problem, seek information from the library, medical or mental health center, family service agency, chemical dependency center, eating disorder clinic, or call 1-800-635-1022 for a free information packet.

EXTENDED CHALLENGE - *If you discover that your eating is a problem, find counseling without delay.*

Excess body fat is a pressing medical problem. Obese people have difficulty exercising. Their heart, lungs and circulation are overburdened and often become impaired. Their hip joints, and especially their knee joints are prone to injury.

If you are even ten pounds overweight, adhere to a sensible and enjoyable nutrition and exercise program. Consult a professional trained in sound nutrition and physical fitness before starting any weight loss program.

EXTENDED CHALLENGE - *Read Covert Bailey's book, Fit or Fat? for ideas how to attain physical fitness and permanent control of excess fat in as little as 12 minutes of aerobic exercise a day.*

Some people are heavy without being overweight because of large bone and muscle mass. Weighing oneself doesn't consider "body type" or the daily changes in body fluids. Find out your ideal body weight given your height and the size of body frame you inherited.

First, determine whether you have a "twiggy to chunky" body structure and accept it. Next, use the chart on the next page to estimate whether you have a weight problem; if you do, eat wisely and exercise soundly.

EXTENDED CHALLENGE - *Learn your percentage of body fat by taking a water buoyancy, electrical impedance, body fat computer, or skin fold (caliper) test. Measuring body fat is more accurate than weighing oneself to determine if there's a problem.*

Height and Weight
Adjusted to Body Frame

Men

Height	Small	Medium	Large
5'2"	128 - 134	131 - 141	138 - 150
5'3"	130 - 136	133 - 143	140 - 153
5'4"	132 - 138	135 - 145	142 - 156
5'5"	134 - 140	137 - 148	144 - 160
5'6"	136 - 142	139 - 151	146 - 164
5'7"	138 - 145	142 - 154	149 - 168
5'8"	140 -148	145 - 157	152 - 172
5'9"	142 - 151	148 - 160	155 - 176
5'10"	144 - 154	151 - 163	158 - 180
5'11"	146 - 157	154 - 166	161 - 184
6'0"	149 - 160	157 - 170	164 - 188
6'1"	152 - 164	160 - 174	168 - 192
6'2"	155 - 168	164 - 178	172 - 197
6'3"	158 - 172	167 - 182	176 - 202
6'4"	162 - 176	171 - 187	181 - 207

Women

Height	Small	Medium	Large
4'10"	102 - 111	109 - 121	118 - 131
4'11"	103 - 113	111 - 123	120 - 134
5'0"	104 - 115	113 - 126	122 - 137
5'1"	106 - 118	115 - 129	125 - 140
5'2"	108 - 121	118 - 132	128 - 143
5'3"	111 - 124	121 - 135	131 - 147
5'4"	114 - 127	124 - 138	134 - 151
5'5"	117 - 130	127 - 141	137 - 155
5'6"	120 - 133	130 - 144	140 - 159
5'7"	123 - 136	133 - 147	143 - 163
5'8"	126 - 139	136 - 150	146 - 167
5'9"	129 - 142	139 - 153	149 - 170
5'10"	132 - 145	142 - 156	152 - 173
5'11"	135 - 148	145 - 159	155 - 176
6'0"	138 - 151	148 - 162	158 - 179

Source of Data - 1979 Build Study of Actuaries and Association of Life Insurance Medical Directors of America 1980

Recipe

for healthy eating...

1. take one fad diet cookbook

2. Shred

3. burn

FAD DIET

ED FISCHER

Beware of "crash" diets which cause people to lose muscle tissue along with fat. After completing these "fad" diets, people tend to regain mostly fat cells; this causes faster weight gain than before the diet. The lasting way to lose weight is through sound eating and exercise.

WELLNESS QUEST™

Review your past week. How often did you exercise? Twelve minutes of aerobic exercise each day is far better than any diet pill. Did you eat balanced meals and reduce calories by eating fewer fatty foods and sweets?

EXTENDED CHALLENGE - *Quit starving yourself! The next time you want to lose excess weight, cut fat from your diet instead of counting calories. In one study, people lost a half pound a week simply by eating 20% to 25% of total calories from fat (instead of their usual 40% of calories from fat).*

ED FISCHER

DIS-ROBE-ICS
GRIN AND BEAR IT

The surest way to form a healthy outlook when gazing into a mirror is through daily aerobic exercise. These steamy workouts raise body heat and burn excess fat. Soft, flabby muscles are toned and body metabolism rises to burn more calories throughout the day.

Start each day with aerobic exercise to raise your metabolism. This allows the body to burn more calories throughout the day. Exercise before eating helps suppress the appetite for greater weight loss.

EXTENDED CHALLENGE - *Follow the guidance of your fitness instructor to tailor an exercise program which fits your personality and schedule. Short aerobic exercises each day will do wonders!*

ED FISCHER

SKIM DOWN

Avoid high-fat dairy foods which raise cholesterol and markedly increase the risk of obesity, heart disease, cancer, and stroke. Persons two years and older are advised to eat "low-fat" dairy foods as a rich source of calcium needed to maintain strong bones.

WELLNESS QUEST™

Choose 1% or 2% milk (skim is better yet), low-fat yogurt, sherbet, ice milk, frozen low-fat yogurt, and low-fat cheeses, (e.g. feta, ricotta, part-skim mozzarella, farmers, romano, and low-fat cottage cheese).

EXTENDED CHALLENGE - *If you choose to eat dairy foods, cut back on whole-milk products, butter, cream, (sweet or sour), ice cream, and high-fat cheeses, (e.g. cheddar, american, brie, swiss, colby, gouda, edam, monterey jack, and cream cheese).*

ED FISCHER

KEEP THE LID ON SATURATED FATS

Mono and poly unsaturated fats will help lower artery-plugging blood cholesterol when they replace highly saturated fats, (see page 26). Cut all fat intake to 30% of total calories, and lower if you are overweight or have high cholesterol.

WELLNESS
QUEST™

Only eat lean cuts of meat today. Avoid hot dogs, bacon, corned beef, sausage, pastrami, spare ribs, organ meats such as liver or kidneys, and ground or luncheon meats with higher fat content.

EXTENDED CHALLENGE - *Avoid non-dairy coffee creamers, sour cream substitutes, and whipped toppings containing coconut or palm oils high in saturated fat.*

Before cooking red meat, trim away all visible fat to lower the calorie and cholesterol content. Eating lean meat (without fat streaks) provides protein, iron, and other nutrients. Grill or broil meat rather than frying it. De-fat gravy by spooning off the refrigerated top layer of fat.

Only eat lean cuts of meat today. Avoid hot dogs, bacon, corned beef, sausage, pastrami, spare ribs, organ meats such as liver or kidneys, and ground or luncheon meats with higher fat content.

EXTENDED CHALLENGE - *Start serving meals without meat; eat no more than 5 to 7 servings of meat a week. Also, get your family accustomed to smaller cuts of meat, (3 to 5 ounces each). Check the label, or ask your butcher for "select" cuts of meat which are the leanest.*

ED FISCHER

FLATULENCE

The average person passes gas about 14 times a day. High gas foods include beans, cabbage, broccoli, brussels sprouts, onions, cauliflower, whole wheat flour, radishes, bananas, apricots, raisons, carrots, bran, pretzels, celery, dairy products and many other nutritious, high-fiber foods.

If you're adding fiber to your diet, start with small amounts over a few weeks until the bowel gets used to it. If you suffer from lactose intolerance, restrict dairy foods, or eat dairy foods with lactase added as advised by your doctor.

EXTENDED CHALLENGE - *Seek medical advice if gas persists. It may signal a problem worth looking into.*

SODIUM IN DIET DRINKS
CAUSES FLUID RETENTION

Feeling like a balloon ready to burst? Sodium in soft drinks and certain sparkling waters might be the cause, along with salted nuts and snacks, canned soups, T.V. dinners, baked goods, cheese, fast foods, cured meats, processed and pickled foods.

Eat fresh, whole fruit and fruit salads with oranges, cantaloupe, strawberries, honeydew, papaya, cherries, peaches, prunes, berries, plums, pineapple, grapefruit, and lemon and lime for extra vitamin C.

EXTENDED CHALLENGE - *When eating salty snack foods, (pretzels, chips) place one serving on your plate; then put the container back into the cupboard to discourage you from taking additional handfuls.*

ED FISCHER

MORE WAYS TO LICK THE SALT HABIT

☐ Taste your food before salting it. Better yet, hide your salt shaker and use herbal seasonings instead.

☐ Use less seasoning salt, soy sauce, bouillon, barbecue sauce, all of which have sodium. Also reduce catsup, steak sauce, chili sauce, cooking wine, and Worcestershire sauce.

☐ Reduce by half, or eliminate completely, salt from recipes when cooking. Cooking water for pasta, vegetables, and rice really doesn't need salt.

☐ Buy unsalted varieties of snack foods rather than salted nuts, crackers, pretzels, and chips.

☐ Avoid sauerkraut, pickles, olives and other foods prepared with salt brine. Cut back all canned vegetables, pickled vegetables, and vegetable juices.

☐ Limit salted, cured, or smoked meat or fish, sardines, kippered herring, lunch meats, hot dogs, and sausage.

☐ Avoid instant packaged soup and salad dressing mixes, dips, and spreads. Select canned soups with reduced sodium.

☐ Increase other minerals such as potassium, calcium, and magnesium from fresh fruits, whole grains and leafy greens and vegetables. Also eat low-fat dairy products and legumes, (beans and peas).

☐ When eating out, ask for french fries without salt, chinese food without MSG, and other foods made to order without salt.

ED FISCHER

FRUIT IS GOOD FOR YOU-
MOST OF THE TIME

Go to the garden of good eating! Eat four or more daily servings of high-energy, low-calorie fruit and vegetable treats to help promote healing, improve regularity, maintain body weight and youthful skin, and boost immunity against diseases, including certain cancers.

Eat fresh, whole fruit and fruit salads with oranges, cantaloupe, strawberries, honeydew, papaya, cherries, peaches, prunes, berries, plums, pineapple, grapefruit, and lemon and lime for extra vitamin C.

EXTENDED CHALLENGE - *Eat other foods rich in Vitamin C each day; green peppers, broccoli, cauliflower, cabbage, tomatoes, brussel sprouts, collard greens, and asparagus are good choices.*

EDFISCHER

WILLIE ADDS FIBER TO HIS DIET

Variety is important when choosing high fiber foods. Soluble fiber helps reduce excess cholesterol and helps control appetite. Insoluble fiber found in whole wheat and other whole grain foods (along with sufficient fluids) helps ease digestion and the elimination of wastes from your body. It may also prevent certain cancers.

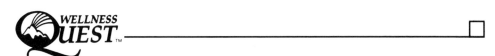

Eat a daily variety of fiber foods like cooked dry beans, dry peas, lentils, brown rice, plain popcorn, and whole grain breads, cereals, crackers, and pasta. Also eat fresh, crunchy fruits and raw, lightly steamed vegetables.

EXTENDED CHALLENGE - *Add fiber to your diet using ideas from the next page. Start slowly and gradually work up to 25 - 35 grams of fiber each day. Spread intake evenly throughout the day.*

TIPS FOR ADDING FIBER TO YOUR DIET

1. Eat a wide variety of fiber foods to help you get both soluble and insoluble fiber. Don't rely only on fiber supplements, or one food.

2. Start adding fiber to your meals slowly; your digestive system needs time to adjust. If fiber is added too rapidly, you may feel bloated or gassy.

3. Drink more fluids, (6 to 8 glasses a day), otherwise fiber can cause constipation.

4. Choose carbohydrates in their natural fibrous coatings; use brown rice instead of white rice. Eat breads, cereals, pastas, and crackers made from whole-grain flour instead of white, refined flour, sometimes referred to as wheat flour.

5. Choose fresh, frozen, or canned vegetables with edible skins and seeds, (e.g. potatoes, cucumbers, beans, peas). Rinse the salt thoroughly from canned vegetables. Avoid those with butter, glaze, sauce, or cheese.

6. Choose fruits with edible skins and seeds, (e.g. apples, dates, strawberries). They can be fresh, frozen, or canned in their own unsweetened juice. Crunchy fruits and vegetables like carrots and apples have 4 to 5 times the fiber of soft foods.

7. Use more cooked dry beans, peas, and lentils to replace the high-fat, no-fiber meats in your diet. Before trying dried beans and peas, start with the more easily digested kinds like lentils, split peas, and lima beans. Eventually work up to navy, pinto, and kidney beans, and dried peas.

8. Add a variety of whole grains to your diet. Find recipes which call for brown rice, barley, bran, bulgur, wheat germ, rye, and corn meal. Be adventuresome.

9. Substitute high-fiber foods for those items you normally eat, especially high-fat foods such as gravies, cream, sauces, and salad dressings. Watch excess pounds disappear.

10. Determine the amount of fiber you eat during the day using the following list showing the average fiber content in one portion of some common foods.

Food	Fiber Content
Fruit	2 grams
Vegetable	2 grams
Starchy Vegetable	3 grams
Legumes	8 grams
Whole grain bread and other whole grain products	2 grams
Cereals	3 grams
Bran cereals	8 grams
Nuts and seeds (1 oz)	3 grams

44

FIBER FEEDBACK

Before you flush, check your stool for fluffies or sinkers. If it floats, you're getting enough dietary fiber and fluids. If it sinks, you're not. "Bowel feedback" may be the most effective way to check whether you're eating enough vegetables, fruits, and whole grain foods.

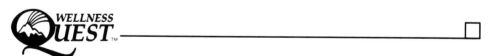

Eat enough fiber, but start out slowly. Too much and you'll blow the lid off the toilet. Keep daily score and alter your diet to achieve the desirable results.

EXTENDED CHALLENGE - *Provide fresh fruits, vegetables, and whole grain breads, cereals, and pastas for yourself and family. Along with the gradual build up of fiber, consume enough fluids (6 to 8 glasses a day) to avoid constipation.*

The Benefits Of Good Eating

☐ higher self-esteem
☐ attract the opposite sex
☐ Clothes fit better
☐ attract the opposite sex
☐ maintain ideal weight
☐ attract the opposite sex
☐ live longer
☐ attract the opposite sex

ED FISCHER

MOST OF ALL, YOU'LL FEEL
BETTER ABOUT YOURSELF

Which area of nutrition on the next page is your weakest? What foods do you need to increase, or cut from your diet? Answer these questions; then make a grocery list based on the information - and stick to it.

EXTENDED CHALLENGE - *Form a "healthy eaters" supper club for people like yourself interested in wholesome food. Swap recipes after enjoying your nutritious meal.*

EAT A WIDE VARIETY OF FOODS
Everyday, eat foods from the four food groups. You'll get calcium, iron, and other essential nutrients.

MAINTAIN HEALTHY WEIGHT
Increase physical activity. Reduce calories by eating less sweets and fatty foods. Lose weight gradually and avoid alcohol.

CHOOSE A DIET LOW IN FAT
Boil, bake or broil — don't fry. Use eggs and organ meats in moderation. Read labels for fat content. Choose lean meats, poultry, fish, dried beans and peas. Limit intake of fats on and in foods.

EAT FRUITS, VEGETABLES AND GRAIN PRODUCTS
Select whole grain breads and cereals. Eat starches rather than fats and sugars. Increase fiber intake with dried beans, peas, nuts, fruits and vegetables.

EAT SUGAR AND SWEETS IN MODERATION
Eat fewer sweets like candy, soft drinks, and cookies. Use less sugar, honey and syrup. Eat fresh fruits whenever possible, or fruits canned in light syrup or their own juices. Recognize other forms of sugar in foods.

USE SODIUM AND SALT IN MODERATION
Reduce salt in cooking; add little to no salt at the table. Read labels for sodium content; limit salty foods.

IF YOU DRINK ALCOHOL, DO SO IN MODERATION
Alcoholic beverages are not part of a healthy diet. Limit all alcoholic beverages to one or two drinks a day. Avoid alcohol if you're pregnant, on certain medications, under legal age, or experience problems when drinking.

BALANCED FOOD

BALANCED YOU!

47

ALCOHOL AND DRUG PROBLEMS

Support yourself through life's hardships. Don't get stuck using alcohol, drugs, or any other senseless crutch which weakens your ability to shoulder responsibility.

ED FISCHER

SLEEPING PILLS CAN BECOME A NIGHTMARE

At times, all people have trouble with light sleep. Causes might include caffeine, nicotine, alcohol, sugar, stress, aging, lack of exercise, some medicines, and going to bed hungry, or, a too full stomach! Over time, sleeping pills can harm sleep and lead to insomnia and drug dependency.

Use natural sleep aids. For instance, try to get to bed at the same time each night, go to bed tired, play soft relaxing music, or read. Try to wake-up the same time every morning, including weekends.

EXTENDED CHALLENGE - *If you can't easily fall asleep or stay asleep throughout the night for a period of three weeks, consult with your physician, or a sleep disorders specialist.*

ED FISCHER

TRANQUILIZERS ONLY GIVE YOU A
TEMPORARY FEELING OF WELL-BEING..

Watch out! Some tranquilizers are addictive. Today, people with anxiety disorders are taught relaxation and living skills. Drug therapy may be needed for chronic mental illness. A doctor trained in the diagnosis and treatment of mental illness decides when this is needed.

WELLNESS QUEST™

Use the right combination of relaxing activities to calm your body and unlock peace of mind. For instance, try taking a walk at dusk or early in the morning. Take mood-altering drugs only when prescribed.

EXTENDED CHALLENGE - *Spend the next few weeks mastering one relaxation skill. Discover the most relaxing way to break from tension (e.g. writing in your diary, drawing nature scenes, blanking your mind, listening to classical music, reading poetry, going barefoot or just bare, stargazing).*

ED FISCHER

ANOTHER CAFFEINE FIEND

Caffeine is one of the most widely used drugs today. It can be a powerful stimulant used to chase away tiredness and sharpen the senses. Too much caffeine can backfire and result in symptoms listed on the next page. Exercise is a far better pick-me-up!

Instead of using caffinated coffee, tea, chocolate and soft drinks to stimulate your body, take a brisk walk, or use other spirited aerobic activities to aerate and refresh yourself!

EXTENDED CHALLENGE - *If caffeine is used to soothe jangled nerves, learn meditation, yoga-style breathing, or progressive muscle relaxation. If you're struggling with caffeine addiction, find a program which counsels, teaches coping skills, and offers nutritional and medical intervention if needed.*

ED FISCHER

CUTTING BACK CAN BE SHAKY

Too much caffeine may cause headaches, nervousness, restlessness, sleeplessness, heartburn, a pounding heart, and frequent trips to the bathroom. Cutting back quickly can produce headaches, depression, and nausea; therefore, a gradual withdrawal is suggested.

Slowly begin to decrease your caffeine use if you have symptoms mentioned above. Herbal tea, caffeine-free pop, sparkling water, or better yet, unsweetened fruit juices and drinking water can be used as caffeine replacements.

EXTENDED CHALLENGE - *Cut caffeine to two or three cups of coffee a day, or its equivalent. Eliminate caffeine altogether if you are pregnant, have ulcers, PMS, panic disorders, or heart-rhythm disorders.*

ED FISCHER

SOME PEOPLE TAKE DRUGS TO BE ONE OF A CROWD

Sure it's important to fit in, but why court death by doing drugs? Win friends and feel connected without chemicals. Use healthy, fun-loving activities to seek peer group pleasure. Then "get high" on each other's spirited fellowship!

Write down the names of your friends. Then ask yourself, " How do these people contribute to my well-being?" If they don't give you reason to feel alive and well, look for new friends who can.

EXTENDED CHALLENGE - *During the next month, search for a group of people who zest for wholesome living. Health clubs, churches, scouts, volunteer organizations, craft or hobby groups, sports teams, service clubs, theatre, dancing, and musical groups may fit the bill. Check out the group and join them if they enliven your spirit.*

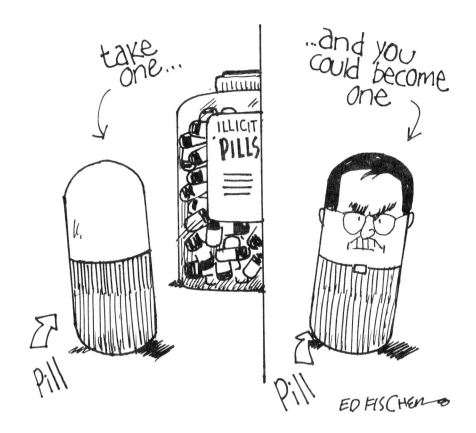

take one...

...and you could become one

ILLICIT PILLS

Pill

Pill

ED FISCHER

Opiate and narcotic drugs are powerfully addicting when abused. Addicts lose interest in daily activities and detach themselves from what's going on. As drug tolerance develops, people take larger doses to avoid withdrawal symptoms.

Only use pain killing drugs that are truly needed as prescribed by your doctor. Obtain medical assistance when any drug causes a degree of irritability, anxiety, or any physical, mental or social problem.

EXTENDED CHALLENGE - *Learn to release endorphins, (your body's natural opiates) as a natural way to relieve pain. Exercise, touch, laughter, crying, and certain music seem to release these powerful pain killers within your body.*

BREAK WITH COCAINE

Crack and cocaine are highly addicting drugs which quickly stimulate the pleasure centers of the brain; shortly after, users' feel intensely depressed and anxious. Even first-time users can suffer seizures, heart attacks, strokes, and death.

Do not risk crack or cocaine for any reason. They are thought to be the most hazardous and compelling drugs today. For information about crack/cocaine and where to get help, call 1-800-COCAINE.

EXTENDED CHALLENGE - *Seek immediate help if you find yourself or a friend in the grips of crack, cocaine, or any other chemical substance.*

SOMEONE WHO GETS STONED MUST HAVE ROCKS IN THE HEAD

Pot is a potent illegal drug which can damage the lungs; it has more cancer-causing chemicals than tobacco. Pot also slows reaction time and coordination, interferes with sex hormones, and changes thought processes including memory, learning, and motivation.

Marijuana is stored in the brain and reproductive organs up to 27 days after use. Questions are being raised about brain and chromosome damage. The best advice today is to avoid marijuana!

EXTENDED CHALLENGE - *If someone trys to coax you to use marijuana, give them the facts, say "No!" and move on to something else. Realize that marijuana is an uncontrolled substance which may be laced with chemicals that add to its danger.*

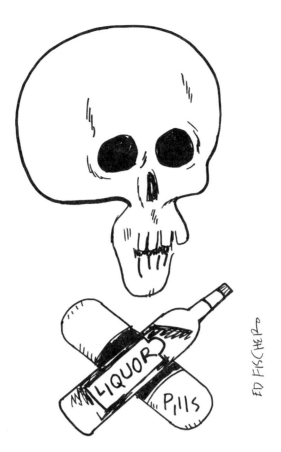

ED FISCHER

THE PARTY'S OVER

When using medicines, always read the directions. Some drugs are deadly when combined with others. Sleeping pills and alcohol are prime examples. Remember, one plus one equals three or more when drugs are combined.

Re-read the labels on your medications today. Avoid alcohol when indicated. The "mix nix" rule applies to alcohol and depressant drugs especially. It's better to be well-read than dead!

EXTENDED CHALLENGE - *Find out from your pharmacist or doctor whether all the medications you are taking are compatible with each other, and with alcohol.*

ED FISCHER

DRINKING AND DRIVING-
A TIME TO GO STRAIGHT!

Alcohol impairs judgement, dulls the senses, and slows reaction speed. No wonder drinking and driving is a deadly combination! Even one or two drinks can throw you off course! Make a pledge to never let yourself, or a friend, drive after drinking!

If you plan to drink alcohol, hand your car keys to a designated alcohol-free driver before you start drinking and still have sound judgement. Insist that your friends do likewise!

EXTENDED CHALLENGE - *Write a pledge never to drink and drive. Ask family members and friends to sign it if they would agree to provide transportation if called upon.*

As with many other diseases, alcoholism may have its origin in the body cells inherited at birth. This means that children who have alcoholic parents or relatives may be more prone to acquire the disease themselves. Watch alcohol research for new findings.

WELLNESS QUEST™

Evaluate your chemical use. Do you detect any problems? Has there been any family member or relative who has had similar problems? Seek advice from a drug counselor or doctor if you discover a pattern.

EXTENDED CHALLENGE - *Seek immediate help for any family member or friend who's having problems with alcohol or drugs. Often times they're not capable of seeing the problem, and it's bound to get worse since alcoholism and chemical dependency are progressive diseases.*

ED FISCHER

If any drug sneaks up and gets you in it's grip, take the first step to regain control; learn the reasons for the chemical problem and seek proper medical treatment. A counselor, pastor, doctor or recovering alcoholic are prepared to help.

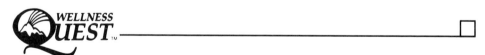

If any drug sneaks up and gets you in it's grip, take the first step to regain control; learn the reasons for the chemical problem and seek proper medical treatment.

EXTENDED CHALLENGE - *Call information for the names and telephone numbers of local support groups, treatment centers, family service centers, or hospitals available to deal with your problem. Determine which organizations would be the most helpful; then call and make an appointment to visit with their representative.*

ED FISCHER

IF YOU WAKE UP IN STRANGE PLACES YOU COULD BE AN ALCOHOLIC!

Know the warning signs of alcoholism. Remember, when people pay an emotional price for a drug user's behavior, it's time to deal with the problem. Don't put up with any person's drug use when you feel put out, upset, ashamed, guilty, or hurt in any way!

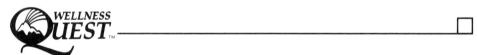

If you are concerned about the ill-effects of someone's drinking, contact your local Alcoholics Anonymous, Alanon, or Alateen group for information. Check the yellow pages, or call information for the telephone number.

EXTENDED CHALLENGE - *Follow the advice given by experts who have years of success treating alcoholism and chemical dependency. Before starting, know the expected benefits, risks, costs, and the alternatives.*

WHEN MILLIE TAKES DRUGS,
SHE FORGETS THINGS...

Blackouts, or not remembering what you've recently done, is a symptom of alcoholism. If you know a drinker who experiences blackouts, or any other symptom of chemical dependency, urge them to see a drug counselor or doctor for an evaluation.

Name two warning signs that a person's alcohol or drug use may be leading to dependency. If you choose to drink alcohol or use other drugs, be aware of these warning signs. (See the next page for the answers.)

EXTENDED CHALLENGE - *Seek help if you detect a problem with your drug use. Likewise obtain help if a family member or friend has a problem.*

HOW TO TELL WHEN DRINKING
IS BECOMING A PROBLEM

To help you decide whether you might have a problem with your drinking, ask yourself the questions below. If you can answer "yes" to any one of these questions, maybe it's time to look at what your drinking might be doing to you.

☐ Do you drink because you have problems? To relax?

☐ Do you drink when you get mad at other people, your friends or parents?

☐ Do you prefer to drink alone, rather than with others?

☐ Are your grades starting to slip? Are you goofing off on your job?

☐ Did you ever try to stop drinking or drink less - and fail?

☐ Have you begun to drink in the morning, before school or work?

☐ Do you gulp your drinks?

☐ Do you ever have loss of memory due to your drinking?

☐ Do you lie about your drinking?

☐ Do you ever get into trouble when you're drinking?

☐ Do you get drunk when you drink, even when you don't mean to?

☐ Do you think it's cool to be able to hold your liquor?

12 Questions from A Message to Teenagers reprinted with permission of Alcoholics Anonymous. A.A. is a program of recovery from alcoholism. Use of this material in connection with any other problem does not imply otherwise.

"BANG!"

In the later stages of chemical dependency, drugs are used to help the addict feel normal. There are medical reasons why an addict is in steady pain and unable to manage his/her mind. Without treatment, serious problems will result. Family members and friends must respond!

Call toll free 1-800-662-HELP for information pertaining to drug abuse and the support groups, treatment centers, and funding programs available in your area.

EXTENDED CHALLENGE - *Be prepared to take decisive action to save the addict. Find out from a chemical dependency counselor how to proceed - then act!*

GET OFF THE UN-MERRY-GO-ROUND

Living with an alcoholic, irrational, or abusive person can leave people feeling dizzy, unsteady, even ill. Support is needed to get off the un-merry-go-round. Small steps can then be taken to focus, get one's bearing, and move towards greater stability.

When your life seems to be in a tailspin, join a support group. Hear what others are doing to keep their feet on the ground. Reach out for the many guiding hands, and hang on!

EXTENDED CHALLENGE - *Remain in your support group, especially when things get better and you're merrily moving along. Your valuable insights and enthusiasm will inspire others. You'll gain respect for caring.*

Get high without drugs or booze; they only blunt the senses and block keen judgement. Host a hearty party and release the playful child inside yourself. Serve your favorite non-alcoholic drinks and feel the natural fiz and sparkle as you frolic

Party alone or with friends. Play cards or be a card; dance wildly; sing your favorite TV commercials; tell jokes, or try talking for 2 or 3 minutes nonstop; see how many compliments you can send in one minute.

EXTENDED CHALLENGE - *Befriend fun-loving people. Playfulness is an important part of recovery from chemical dependency. It takes time for the addict's body to supply the chemical regulators needed to produce the happy feelings of natural euphoria. In the meantime, associate with high-spirited people.*

TOBACCO TROUBLES

Whether you enjoy tobacco, or are the victim of another person's sidestream smoke, use the following ideas to deal with the harmful effects of this addicting drug.

ED FISCHER

Does it look strange? Would you wonder why a person would insert a cigarette into his ear when it could break the ear drum and impair hearing? Do you wonder why people put cigarettes between their lips and suck in hundreds of noxious, filthy, toxic gases?

─── □

Imagine you meet an intelligent being from another planet and are asked to explain why some earthlings put cigarettes into their mouths and suck in poisonous gases. Go ahead and explain the logic.

EXTENDED CHALLENGE - *If you're a tobacco user, write a complete list of reasons why an intelligent being uses tobacco; then write reasons against using tobacco and compare the lists. Post the lists in a visible location.*

─── □

Huge sums of money go up in smoke on tobacco products. Also, much is spent on cleaning soiled clothes, carpets, and curtains, or cosmetic costs for skin damage, and on higher health, car and life insurance. Staggering medical costs result from tobacco related illness and disease.

If you're a tobacco user, make a list of five things you would buy with $100-$300 saved each month by not using tobacco. Post this list in a visible spot, (e.g. in front of the TV set).

EXTENDED CHALLENGE - *If you're a tobacco user, burn a dollar bill each time you chew or light up. Watch your money go up in smoke.*

Smoking is one hobby which leaves you breathless. Tobacco tar attacks the thin air sacs within the lungs. As a result, smokers may develop emphysema, lung cancer, and other disabling and deadly lung diseases. Quitting tobacco may help restore the lungs.

WELLNESS QUEST™ ───

Fill your lungs with air. Now hold all of that air inside while you continue to breath and sense what emphysema feels like. Think of how smoking ruins lungs and lives; resolve not to smoke.

EXTENDED CHALLENGE - *If you use tobacco, write the following statement each time you use, "I can quit - I will quit - I quit!"*

PEOPLE WERE RIGHT, CIGARETTE BREATH CAN STOP A BUFFALO!

Smoker's lose their keen sense of taste and smell. This often makes them unaware of how bad "tobacco breath" really is. Add to this the awful tobacco odor on clothes, hair and skin. No wonder many people have difficulty getting close to tobacco users.

The next time a tobacco user's breath bothers you, kindly tell them, "I'm finding the tobacco on your breath bothersome." Then move away, or offer them a sugarless breath mint or piece of gum.

EXTENDED CHALLENGE - *If you're a tobacco user, brush your teeth and tongue after each use to remove the odorous tar and sweeten your breath.*

To a kisser, a mouth with snuff may seem like a cesspool of drool. In addition to foul breath, chewing or dipping tobacco is seen as offensive. The practice is highly addicting and causes health risks including tooth decay, gum disease, high blood pressure, and various cancers.

If you chew tobacco, realize how offensive others may view your habit. If that doesn't convince you to quit, consider the health risks; then make a commitment to give up tobacco - and do it.

EXTENDED CHALLENGE - *Share your honest concerns with a family member or friend who chews or dips tobacco. Without preaching, tell them specifically why you're concerned, and that you're willing to support their efforts to quit, if they are willing.*

ED FISCHER

"CO-WORKERS ALLOW A SMOKER ONE MORE CIGARETTE"

Don't shoot! Be sensitive and caring toward tobacco addicts. Use gentle ways to express your concern. Nicotine addiction is one of the very toughest drugs to conquer. Your understanding and encouragement may help inspire the addict to quit.

If you smoke, respect the health of your co-workers, friends, and family by not smoking in their presence. Refuse to smoke in your home or car.

EXTENDED CHALLENGE - *Work to get a non-smoking environment at work. Insist that lunch rooms, bathrooms, elevators, work areas and corridors are smoke-free. Provide a smoking area outside the building like many other worksites (and homesites) do.*

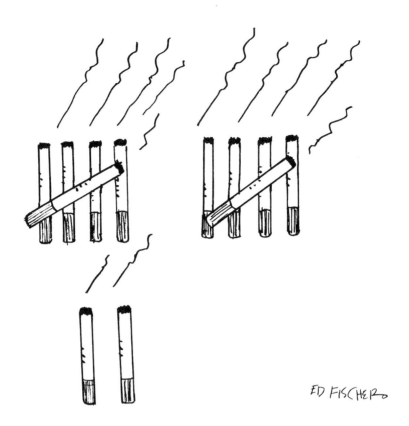

ED FISCHER

DAYS OFF YOUR LIFE...

Tobacco use adds up to loss of life. Over 350,000 Americans will die this year of tobacco related diseases. That's more Americans than were killed in all the wars fought this century. Tobacco kills 13 times as many Americans as hard drugs and 8 times as many as auto accidents. The worldwide cost in lives now approaches 2.5 million per year.

Identify three things you would like to do in the final 7 years of your life. Compare that with lying in a cemetery. Also, name three people who would miss you if you died 7 years earlier than expected.

EXTENDED CHALLENGE - *Once and for all, resolve to quit tobacco. Set a date two weeks from today. Record each time you use tobacco with a check mark on a piece of paper tucked in the wrapper of your cigarette pack. Consider each mark as possible days off your life.*

There are two ways to quit tobacco; one of them leaves you cold. The other way renews the senses and extends life. People need to ask whether quitting tobacco is worth living for? Or, is using tobacco worth dying for?

Think of a friend, co-worker, family member, relative, or celebrity who died prematurely because of tobacco. What would they say about their tobacco use? What would they say about your tobacco use?

EXTENDED CHALLENGE - *Collect your cigarette butts in a "butt bottle" to show how much you smoked in the final two weeks. View each butt as another reason to quit once and for all. Use ideas on the next page to kick the habit.*

ED FISCHER

WAYS TO QUIT TOBACCO

Whether you chew or dip tobacco, or smoke cigarettes, pipes or cigars, there are countless health benefits for quitting. Here are several approaches to consider.

1. Call the American Lung Association office closest to you and inquire about their "Freedom From Smoking" sessions in your area. Ask about the program cost and course description. Also request free information packets containing effective ways to quit tobacco on your own.

2. Compare the ALA program to the tobacco cessation programs offered by hospitals and clinics in your area. What type of behavior modification techniques do these program use? What percentage of participants don't use tobacco one year after completing their program?

3. If you're strongly addicted to nicotine, consult with your physician about "nicotine reduction therapy" to help cope with nicotine withdrawal. Chewing Nicorette (a gum containing nicotine, available by prescription) may reduce nicotine cravings and reduce the anxiety, irritability, headaches, and other symptoms of nicotine withdrawal.

    Studies have shown that combining Nicorette with reputable stop-smoking programs can triple the chances for success.

4. Take action! Follow through with your desire to quit tobacco. Before long, you'll make tobacco disappear the healthy way - by trashing it. This sleight-of-hand trick reduces health risks and increases the magical wonder-workings of a healthy body.

LITE UP....

ED FISCHER

WITHOUT CIGARETTES...

Lighten up! No more dirty looks, snide remarks, or healthy people hassling you. No more rushing your meals for a smoke or avoiding your non-smoking friends out of shame for your habit! You are home free; the tobacco monkey is off your back!

Today, find wholesome ways to ignite your energy and spark your spirit without tobacco or other drugs. Walk in the woods, fly a kite, play a sport, or do other lighthearted fresh-air activities.

EXTENDED CHALLENGE - *Quit tobacco for good! Refuse to accept the following excuses. "I've tried to quit before, it's too difficult." or, "If I quit, I'll gain weight." or, "Tobacco won't hurt me, I know lots of tobacco users who are healthy." or, "I need cigarettes to relax." These claims are lame excuses. Decide to quit - then do it!*

Raw carrot sticks satisfy oral cravings. These tasty tidbits don't cause cancer, heart disease, stroke, bad breath, yellow teeth, or carrot stick fits. Best of all, you won't need to ask, "What's up doc?"

Treat yourself to raw carrot sticks today. Enjoy the crisp, crunchy texture and the clean fresh taste. If you have a friend who smokes or chews tobacco, offer them some.

EXTENDED CHALLENGE - *Celery sticks and plastic straws can also be chewed to satisfy oral cravings as you work to quit tobacco. Avoid chewing tooth picks, as splinters can cause damage if swallowed.*

ED FISCHER

STOP SMOKING....
THEN WATCH YOUR SMOKE

Carbon monoxide makes people feel laid back because of the oxygen lack. Exercise does the opposite; it produces energy due to the oxygen gain and floods the body with endorphins, the body's natural pain killer which "mellows" the person while creating the runners' high.

WELLNESS QUEST™

Avoid carbon monoxide from exhaust and tobacco smoke. Ask to sit in the non-smoking section in restaurants and at work. Breathing in sidestream smoke risks health and dampens your energy glow!

EXTENDED CHALLENGE - *If you're quitting tobacco, substitute exercise for smoking. For example, walk instead of smoking after dinner. Much like tobacco, exercise stimulates the adrenal glands and releases blood sugar, however without the toxic gases.*

STRESSED
OUT

Feeling hampered by deadlines and obligations? Stress can cause an assortment of illnesses and make you a basket case. Used properly, stress can make life enjoyable and fulfilling.

ED FISCHER

STRESSED FOR SUCCESS

Feeling over-stressed and off balance? Perhaps you are trying to handle too many things at once. To manage excess stress, cut back your activities and try focusing on one task at a time. Notice how enjoyable life becomes as you lighten the load.

Make a list of all the things you plan to do today, including family and fitness activities. Number them according to their importance, then do the most urgent ones first. Enjoy!

EXTENDED CHALLENGE - *Schedule leisure-time activities for the upcoming week by writing down your plans, then carrying them out.*

ED FISCHER

A HALF BAKED IDEA OF
WHAT LIFE'S ALL ABOUT

When you feel like a dud because you're a spud
stuffed in your easy chair,
kick yourself free from that blasted T.V.
and "exercise" body care!

Lack of exercise stresses the body. Limit television watching to one hour or less today. Exercise during your free time and feel body stress melt away as energy is restored. See "Special Note" on page 20.

EXTENDED CHALLENGE - *Stretch, walk in place, and do sit-ups during commercials if you're watching TV more than an hour a day. Exercise each day during a program you regularly watch.*

ED FISCHER

WINNER AND STILL CHUMP!

Some people are hard on themselves. They demand the impossible, then demean themselves for not delivering! They need to hang up their gloves and retire from the stressful arena of self put-downs.

Score a TKO by "Taking the Kindness Oath"! Any time you're tempted to knock yourself for failing, praise yourself for trying instead. At the end of the day, review all of your winning thoughts!

EXTENDED CHALLENGE - *Get into the habit of reciting your winning thoughts at bedtime and again in the morning.*

ED FISCHER

As information keeps expanding, we need to realize that learning facts today is not as important as knowing how to think. There are many ways to show our thinking skills, such as music, sports, drawing, cooking, reading, fixing, and relating to others.

If feeling dumb is your rule of thumb, think of one wholesome skill you're good at. Consider at least three skills required to perform that activity; then feel proud of what you can do!

EXTENDED CHALLENGE - *Feel a greater sense of accomplishment as you continue to practice and improve your skill.*

ED FISCHER

BE YOURSELF

In the desire to be liked, people pretend to be someone they are not. Their behavior is seen as phoney and often creates stress for themselves and their viewing audience. Not being oneself is hard work and burns energy which could be used to refine a skill or develop a hobby.

 WELLNESS QUEST™

Pinpoint one thing you do which makes you appear phoney. Consider what might happen if you eliminate this behavior and act natural. Next, make this change and notice how people respond.

EXTENDED CHALLENGE - *Ask a friend what they like best about you. Be willing to share your positive impressions of them.*

ED FISCHER

Don't fall for a sweet sounding person or group without first looking ahead and considering where you're headed. With a clear view of the future, pay attention to what's in your best interest. It may be wiser to proceed alone, or move in different directions.

WELLNESS
QUEST™

Recall one time you wisely stood up for yourself when pleasing others would have been simpler - that took courage! Praise yourself for taking steps which set you apart. Good going!

EXTENDED CHALLENGE - *Praise a family member, friend, co-worker, or fellow student for one quality or action which shows their individuality. Specifically tell them what you admire. Let them know why you hold them in high esteem.*

Call it procrastination, the disease of delay. Symptoms include laziness and heaps of guilt. People can easily overcome this idle condition; after all, no one is glued to the starting blocks. To forge ahead, simply get on track by taking the first step!

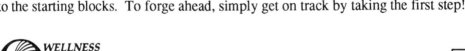

Today, think of one thing you've put off doing. Now, stand up, walk towards the project, lay your hands on it, and begin. Work ten minutes, then look back and see what you've accomplished!

EXTENDED CHALLENGE - *Repeat this ten minute "hands on" approach each day until the project is completed. Chances are good that ten minutes of work mushrooms into longer stints of labor every now and then. Try it and see!*

Unrelieved stress can build up within the body to block energy, tighten muscles, constrict blood vessels, and cause a host of ailments including headaches, muscular pain, dizziness, high blood pressure, tiredness, indigestion, constipation, and many more.

Take an inventory of your aches and pains. If they seem stress related, find ways to balance stress with relaxation, (e.g. enjoy a Gary Larson, Dave Barry, or other humorous book), listen to a relaxing tape, or use other relaxing activities.

EXTENDED CHALLENGE - *If your symptoms persist, seek medical advice from a doctor who's in tune with your lifestyle and interested in your total well-being.*

O.K. You've punched Frosty's pipe through his water-logged brain: big deal! At least no one's hurt! The same is true when you pound a pillow, or smash tennis balls with vengeance. It's healthy to get "angry" energy out of the body, providing no one's harmed in the process.

Blow off steam using vigorous exercise; then ease your mind by viewing the incident as a "learning experience". If that doesn't work, talk with someone who can suggest alternate ways to view the situation.

EXTENDED CHALLENGE - *Upset with a family member or friend? Discuss the situation, calmly listen to each other, decide on a mutually agreed upon solution, try it out. If the first solution doesn't fit, try another. Then reward yourselves for using anger in a constructive manner!*

Here's the low-down on boredom. Only one person can bore you. Guess who? Accepting that fact is the first step out of the doldrums. The next step is taking total responsibility to de-bore yourself by stimulating your mind when doing humdrum work.

Freshen your stale routine. When listening to a tedious lecture, take notes using colorful pens; draw and doodle freely. Think of other creative ways to overcome your boredom without causing problems.

EXTENDED CHALLENGE - *Each day, look for a novel way to change your routine, (e.g. sit in a different seat at the dinner table, take a different route home after work, eat with your opposite hand, listen to an unfamiliar radio program).*

Depressed feelings can result from one's outlook on life. It can also be caused by diet, lack of exercise, medical reasons, or one's ways of handling stress. Chronic or major depression is an illness which requires therapy and, at times, medication.

WELLNESS QUEST™

Whenever feeling depressed, take proper steps to treat it. For example, take spirited walks, skip salty snacks, eat wholesome food, think of the bright side of life, and avoid alcohol, soft drinks, and other sweets.

EXTENDED CHALLENGE - *If symptoms last two weeks or longer, seek a medical opinion since the cause may be medical in nature.*

WARNING SIGNS

If you experience two or more of the following symptoms for two weeks or longer, you could be suffering from some form of depressive or mental illness. These illnesses have physical or medical origins and can be successfully treated in nearly 80% of all cases with therapy and, at times, medication. Help is needed from a professional trained in the diagnosis and treatment of mental illness.

☐ Changes in personality or mood

☐ Withdrawal from others: abnormal self-centeredness

☐ Confused thinking or unusual fixed false beliefs
(i.e. someone is out to get you)

☐ Strange or grandiose ideas

☐ Too much worry, anxiety, sadness, fear, hopelessness

☐ Changes in eating or sleeping patterns

☐ Difficulty in coping with daily activities

☐ Emotions that are inappropriate to the situation
(laughing at a loved one's funeral)

☐ Denial of obvious problems

☐ Increased use of alcohol or other drugs

☐ Violent or suicidal thoughts or actions

☐ Anger or hostility not right for the situation

☐ Seeing or hearing things in ways that others do not

ED FISCHER

Everyone has mood swings, and some feelings are more intense than others. Remember, it's time to make lifestyle changes when your feelings cause problems for anyone. Medical help is needed when the mood swings are the result of mental or physical illness.

Tonight, review how you were feeling today. Did you create any mood which was harmful to yourself or others? If so, picture yourself handling the situation in a better way; such mental practice can be helpful.

EXTENDED CHALLENGE - *Talk with a counselor if upsetting feelings regularly cause pain for yourself or others. Be open and honest in doing so.*

Caffeine, nicotine, sugar, pep pills, and other stimulants stress the body and can leave you feeling depressed when coming down. Exercise, singing, and laughter are a few natural ways to perk up the body, and they don't leave you feeling flat afterwards!

When feeling sluggish today, rub or clap your hands together and repeat vigorously, "I'm excited about what I'm doing!" Pep yourself up using this zestful thought and vigorous body action; then feel excited!

EXTENDED CHALLENGE - *Consider which family member or friend peps you up. Get together often and share their exuberance.*

Looking for ways to glow? Yearning to dazzle people, or impress yourself? Perhaps your brilliant efforts cast a negative spell and cause life to lose its luster. What price are you willing to pay for your behavior in terms of friendship and well-being?

Make a list of 5 or more behaviors which you enjoy; then identify which ones tarnish life in any way. Consider whether it's in your best interest to continue those behaviors, or give them up.

EXTENDED CHALLENGE - *Eliminate any behavior which seems too costly in terms of time, money, self-worth, or relationships. Seek professional help, or join a support group if you're unable to overcome the compulsion yourself.*

ED FISCHEN

Lighten up! Discard any oversized and outdated worries which burden you. Give up the "griefcase" of past problems which needlessly consumes energy. Refuse to be hampered by previous mistakes. Instead, fill your hope chest with new plans for a happy future.

 **WELLNESS QUEST**™

The next time you fret over a problem, ask yourself, "Is this worth worrying about?" If so, take time to figure out a solution - then take action. If the problem isn't worth brooding over, forget it!

EXTENDED CHALLENGE - *Don't gunnysac - that is, avoid mentioning unrelated problems when discussing a dispute. Digging up past difficulties to support your point of view makes people defensive. It's more effective to narrow the focus on matters at hand.*

ED FISCHER

LAUGHTER IS GOOD FOR YOU, AT THE RIGHT TIME

Does your ready-wit raise people's spirits? Or does it put them down? Humor has many health-boosting benefits, if your remarks are right for the situation. Pay attention to your humorous words and funny antics. Do they fracture, or foster friendship?

Find wholesome ways to laugh today. For example, wear a clown's nose to work (at least on the bus going to work); tell a friend about a recently embarrassing incident; watch the playful antics of an animal or young child.

EXTENDED CHALLENGE - *See how many days in a row you can make at least one person laugh out loud, (tickling not allowed). Once you establish a record, outdo yourself.*

Are you racing around without getting anywhere? Is your life in a tailspin, out of control? Perhaps it's time to go to a secluded spot and examine what's driving you. Determine whether your life seems headed in the right direction. If not, decide what new paths to take.

Spend at least twenty minutes alone. Quietly reflect on your past week. Are you spending quality time each day with family and friends. If you're too busy, consider what changes need to be made?

EXTENDED CHALLENGE - *Sit down with family and friends and discuss ways to spend more meaningful time together. First determine what activities people enjoy; then make plans to share time together doing these things.*

LOSE YOURSELF IN FAMILY PLAY

Exercise your tomfoolery! Take part in sports, entertainment, hobbies, or any merrymaking, hob-and-nob activities which cause laughter. Notice how close family members feel when fun times and good cheer are shared by all. Go ahead, raise the roof - get carried away with wholesome fun!

Spend at least 30 minutes today with family members playing a game, sport, hobby, or goofing around. Don't keep score, just play for the fun of it! Enjoy the closeness and high spirits which ensue.

EXTENDED CHALLENGE - *Each week, let family members take turn selecting a fun activity, (e.g. horseshoes, camping, sewing a family quilt, racing a stockcar, making a music video, going to a movie). Choose activities which can be enjoyed be all. Everyone pitch in and play.*

PUT YOURSELF ON CLOUD 9

Take time out from tension with soothing mental journeys to your most peaceful place. Take deep breaths, smile inwardly, and experience total calm as you quietly visualize your quiet scene. Feel restored as your tension slowly slips away.

Close your eyes for several minutes and picture yourself enjoying your most relaxing place. Pay attention to details and breath in the fresh air. Feel the soft, warm, peaceful feelings which flood your body.

EXTENDED CHALLENGE - *When you can't be there, travel in your mind to lush tropical forests. Feel serene watching a spectacular sunset unfold. Gaze at untamed waterfalls and bold mountain ranges peering through the clouds. Take mini-mental vacations and go anywhere you fancy.*

ENVIRONMENTAL SENSITIVITY

Would your body be government approved? Lead in pipes, radon, toxic wastes, air pollution, pesticides on foods, impure water, leaching tooth amalgams, radiation, asbestos, tobacco smoke, interactive drugs, and other exposures may be spoiling your contents.

Go beyond wishful thinking. Invest time and energy to make your dream of a clean and healthy environment come true. Start by making small changes to clean-up and beautify your surroundings.

Starting with your bedroom, then moving to other rooms, clean, dust, and straighten up. Use nontoxic cleaners. Donate unused clothes, appliances and other items to those in need.

EXTENDED CHALLENGE - *Once your living quarters are clean, move outside and tidy up the grounds surrounding your home. If needed, form a neighborhood green committee to help pick up litter and beautify the area.*

PEOPLE WHO DON'T RECYCLE

Green consumers practice the 3 R's: "refuse, reuse, and recycle". Refuse to buy environmentally unsafe products, reuse as often as possible before throwing away, and recycle whenever you can. The aftermath of your efforts is reduced damage to our earth.

Look for the recycled symbol (a triangle of arrows) when buying a product. Reuse your paper grocery bags or use a canvas or string bag for your shopping. Recycle glass, paper and aluminum.

EXTENDED CHALLENGE - *Play an active role at school or work - make sure boxes are stationed at convenient locations to collect all white scrap paper and discarded aluminum cans and bottles. Make sure fluorescent bulbs are used to replace incandescent bulbs.*

Today's children will inherit either a wholesome earth, or one which is poisoned. Individual actions will determine future air, land, and water quality. Never before has so much depended on the combined efforts of individuals.

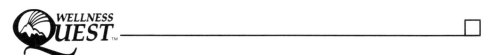

Work as a family to reduce electrical usage at home. Plan to spend money saved on the electric bill on leisure time activities. Start by turning off lights in rooms not being used and replacing light bulbs with low watt bulbs (better yet, flourescent ones).

EXTENDED CHALLENGE - *Attempt to set new records each month for the lowest electrical bill. Learn to enjoy darkened rooms and hallways. Know that behind each shadow there's a bright goal - to save the earth's resources. Look for other ways to conserve energy by using less gas and water at home.*

A typical child soils 7,500 diapers before being potty trained. Over 18 billion dirty diapers are tossed out every year in the USA. Plastic diapers don't biodegrade completely and are slowly filling our landfills. You and your baby must stop this waste!

Hire an inexpensive diaper service rather than using disposable diapers. Buy eggs in old-fashioned cardboard cartons instead of styrofoam ones; eat ice milk or frozen yogurt from a cone instead of a polystyrene dish or waxed-paper cup.

EXTENDED CHALLENGE - *Purchase fresh fruit juices in recyclable or returnable glass bottles instead of plastic ones. Buy fresh fruit and vegetables whenever possible instead of canned or frozen packages. Make sure your old trade-in tires won't be dumped in a landfill.*

WHAT OZONE PROBLEM

The writing is on the wall! Unless lifestyle habits are changed, sunny "death ray" days loom ahead. The ozone layer protecting the earth from ultraviolet radiation is being depleted. Marine life, crop damage, immune system suppression, eye damage, and skin cancer will increase.

Avoid products containing methyl chloroform, (certain glues, flea and roach killers, art supplies, varnishes, auto cleaning sprays, lubricants, nail polish, carpet and fabric cleaners, aerosol spray cans.)

EXTENDED CHALLENGE - *Reduce ozone-depleting freon by opening windows and using fans, instead of air conditioning your home and car. If your air conditioner or refrigerator leaks, get it fixed by a person using a vampire machine designed to capture freon.*

What's odorless, invisible, deadly and creeping into homes? Radon - a radioactive gas which has affinity to lung tissue and causes lung cancer. Certain areas in the country, (perhaps your locality) have high levels of radon. Find out if you're at risk.

Call your county health department and ask if your area is at risk. If there is a problem, purchase a radon detection kit and test your basement for radon.

EXTENDED CHALLENGE - *Take appropriate action if radon is detected in your home. Install the recommended ventilation system and urge your friends to check their basement.*

PRACTICE WHAT YOU PREACH

You can talk the talk, but do you walk the walk? Does your concern for the environment fall in step with daily action? Take an honest look at your day-to-day practices; then make necessary adjustments to help preserve our earth.

Read through the list on the next page. Place a check mark on each item you regularly do. Work to include the other ideas in your daily routine. Whenever possible, influence others living close to you to join in.

EXTENDED CHALLENGE - *Expand your knowledge and concern for the environment by joining World Watch Institute, Box 6991, Syracuse New York, 13217-9942. For $15 a year, you'll receive a bi-monthly periodical intune with current problems and solutions.*

SAVE THE EARTH

- ☐ Use cold or warm water when washing clothes whenever possible.
- ☐ Use old newspaper to clean windows and mirrors, or as packaging material.
- ☐ Use low-flow aerators on shower heads and faucets to save water.
- ☐ Place a brick inside the toilet tank to save water on each flush.
- ☐ Shovel snow and use sand on ice instead of salt.
- ☐ Close the drapes over windows to insulate the house from heat or cold.
- ☐ Use rechargeable batteries rather than buying new ones.
- ☐ Plant a tree in your yard each year; also plant a garden.
- ☐ Turn down your water heater. Wrap the heater in an insulating sleeve.
- ☐ Pull the plug when not watching TV to save on standby power.
- ☐ Turn off burners on the electric range minutes before you're done cooking.
- ☐ Obey speed limits and don't race your car engine.
- ☐ Set up a magazine pool to swap/share magazines with friends.
- ☐ Thaw out frozen foods before cooking them.
- ☐ Clean glass with 3 tbsp. white vinegar to one quart of water.
- ☐ Leave spiders do their work in your home killing insects.
- ☐ Use verbal communication instead of written notes.
- ☐ Shut off your car engine when stuck in traffic for 60 seconds or longer.
- ☐ Remove damp clothes from the dryer and hang them to dry.
- ☐ Wear sweaters and keep the thermostat at 65 degrees or lower in the winter.
- ☐ Use returnable glass pop or milk bottles instead of plastic ones.
- ☐ Borrow or share appliances and tools you use infrequently.

ACID RAIN

Rain, snow, fog or mist contaminated with sulfur dioxide and nitrogen oxide is slowly killing aquatic plants. Fish are dying as toxic mercury levels rise. Forests die in the corrosive drizzle; soil quality declines. We've danced around the acid rain problem long enough!

 **WELLNESS QUEST**™ ———————————————————————— ☐

Ride your bicycle or walk instead of taking short car trips to the store, to school, to work, or a friend's house. Ride mass transit, or form a car pool rather than driving alone. Keep your car engine tuned and the tires properly inflated.

EXTENDED CHALLENGE - *When buying a car, select one which is most fuel-efficient. Not only will you save money on gasoline, you'll be saving the environment. The auto industry will respond by manufacturing more fuel-efficient cars as the demand increases.*

☐

ED FISCHER

THERE ARE SIGNS THAT WE ARE CONTAMINATING OUR WATER

Prevent poisons from seeping into the ground water. Don't throw away leftover paint, oil, gas, bug and weed killer, oven cleaner, nail polish remover, batteries of all sizes, and other harsh chemicals that are dumped and soon seep into our drinking water.

Call your local Health Department today and ask for the correct way to throw away containers that hold leftover chemicals. Buy only smaller amounts of needed chemicals and use them all up.

EXTENDED CHALLENGE - *Conserve water. Limit showers to 2 or 3 minutes, turn off the faucet when rinsing dishes, limit or eliminate lawn watering, sweep rather than hose sidewalks clean, and don't flush the toilet unnecessarily.*

BE ONE WITH NATURE

Take in the beauty and richness of nature, or... absorb the polluted, barren earth. Being in tune with nature means creating harmony with the sky, air, water, plants, and creatures - for better, or worse. Will this union enrich life, or make both of you sick?

Sit under a tree, lie on the grass (or snow), and watch the clouds drift by as you contemplate your oneness with nature. Consider one way to show your affection towards nature before the day ends - then do it.

EXTENDED CHALLENGE - *Spend time outdoors for the sole purpose of enjoying nature. Marvel at the gentle, sweeping motion of trees in the wind; experience the breathtaking view of spectacular sunsets; delight in the playful antics of wildlife. Know that you are one with the mother of all mothers.*

only YOU can set a fire under your congressman

ED FISCHER

Tell legislators who make the "laws of the land," that they'll lose their seat in congress if they're more interested in saving their careers than in saving lives. Sway legislative thinking and spark action towards sound environmental laws through informed letter writing and earnest phone calls.

WELLNESS QUEST™

Join an environmental organization or green group within your community, (e.g. Sierra Club, Issac Walton League). You'll acquire factual information and a group identity which can help influence lawmakers.

EXTENDED CHALLENGE - *Expand your knowledge of environmental concerns. Purchase Will Steger's new broad range book entitled Saving the Earth, published by Random House. The book provides excellent illustrations and practical suggestions for individual and community action.*

EXERCISE
BODY CARE

Propel yourself along the highway of health. Experience strength and vitality in all of its glory. Feel the joy and peace resulting from spirited exercise.

ED FISCHER

ED FISCHER

USE IT OR LOSE IT

Physical activity helps you gain and then keep muscle strength and bone thickness. Without exercise, muscles weaken and bones grow thinner. Walking, swimming, dancing, wheelchair exercises all help prevent muscle loss, osteoporosis, and obesity.

 WELLNESS QUEST™ ————————————————————————————————————— ☐

Play it safe. Check with your physician before starting any new exercise program, especially if you are over 40, out of shape, or have any medical condition. It may be unnecessary, but do it just to be safe.

EXTENDED CHALLENGE - *Befriend a person who's interested in exercising with you at your pace. Make a commitment to exercise together for at least for two weeks. Enjoy each other's company and the gradual feeling of fitness which develops.*

——————————————————————————————————————— ☐

ED FISCHER

WALKING IS GOOD EXERCISE, BUT WATCH WHERE YOU'RE GOING

Exercise "care" while working out! Find a safe time and place. Then, work out at a pace which allows you to carry on casual conversation. Experience "low impact pleasure" as you boost your energy, and feel more fully alive and alert!

WELLNESS QUEST™ ——————————————————————————————————□

Schedule fitness into your daily routine. For example, park your car, or get off the bus early, and walk one or two miles to and from work or school each day. Choose parking spaces farthest from the entrance when shopping.

EXTENDED CHALLENGE - *Over the next six weeks, increase your walking from 12 minutes a day to 30 minutes or longer. Begin to walk with greater intensity as you improve your fitness.*

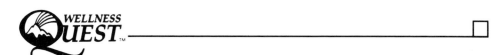

ED FISCHER

ARF-RO-BICS
FOR A LASTING IMPRESSION

O.K. So your mad dash into a new fitness program became a pain in the b _ _ _.
Forget that unfortunate experience.   Condition your body as you would train a
puppy, with gentle persistence. Make no bones about it, in time you'll feel fitter
than fido.

Start a new fitness program. Make each workout comfortable for the first few
weeks - do only half of what you're capable. To be safe, consult a fitness expert
if you have a medical condition, or are just beginning.

EXTENDED CHALLENGE - *Since you're starting a new fitness program,*
why not ask a family member or friend to join you? Both of you can encourage
each other and enjoy spirited conversations during the fun times together.

WHEN EXERCISING
STAY IN YOUR COMFORT ZONE

Exercise smart! Sweat easy! Enjoy workouts which slowly build your strength, flexibility, and fitness of your heart, lungs, and circulatory system. Select exercises which work your body, yet ones which can be repeated the next day in comfort.

Be body wise! Stop exercising when you experience nausea, chest pain, dizziness, breathlessness, fatigue, or other symptoms of distress. Be attentive! Heed these warnings to slow down!

EXTENDED CHALLENGE - *Chat with your exercise partners while working out to ensure that you're not overdoing it. If you're unable to carry on a comfortable conversation, slow down!*

BUILD FLEXIBILITY

Stretching keeps muscles supple and joints limber thereby preventing injury and slowing the aging process. Flexibility exercise also tones muscles, builds strength, and increases the range of easy motion allowing you to move more gracefully.

Slowly move your major muscles and joints through a natural range of easy stretching motion for ten minutes daily. Hold each position for 15 to 30 seconds; avoid sudden or bouncing movements.

EXTENDED CHALLENGE - *Start each day with a series of stretches. Use them to "warm up" and "cool down" before and after exercise and athletics. Stretch a few minutes every hour you sit. Finally, at the end of each day, honor your body with slow, reflective stretches.*

USE PHYSICAL ACTIVITY
AS A MEANS OF RISK AND THRILL

Adventure at every turn!   The primal excitement of hunting hairy mammoths and wooly rhinos... the zeal of knights jousting before the Queen... . Sports provide the risk and thrill of daring exploits which tickle and excite the human core.

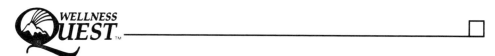

Consider your age and physical ability, then discover a new sport which stirs your senses and creates physical fireworks. Take a healthy risk; sign up for a sport you haven't tried before, then excite yourself!

EXTENDED CHALLENGE - *Entice a family member or friend to join you in the new sporting endeavor. Buy or borrow needed equipment, obtain proper instruction - then have a blast!*

TUNE UP YOUR CAR   TONE UP YOUR BODY

Feeling sluggish? Enhance your performance with premium fuel, (eat wholesome food); keep fluid levels up, (drink 6-8 glasses a day); work your motor muscles with exercise, (don't stay idle too long). Soon your body will be fine-tuned and ready to excel!

WELLNESS QUEST™

Instead of taking the car or bus for short one- or two-mile trips, ride your bicycle or walk. Know that you are helping your car, strengthening your body, and saving our environment!

EXTENDED CHALLENGE - *Do you spend as much time and money each month caring for your body, as you spend maintaining your family car? If not, consider investing in a health club membership and athletic equipment. Then workout to keep yourself running smoothly.*

ED FISCHER

Don't be a cream puff prone to injury. Build fiber! Strengthen your muscles to improve posture, coordination, appearance, energy levels, and self-esteem. To avoid injury, obtain the guidance of a physical educator or exercise therapist before starting any new exercise program.

Obtain proper instruction, then spend ten minutes every other day building strength in your legs, arms, neck, shoulders, abdomen and back. Feel how physical strength firms your mental backbone!

EXTENDED CHALLENGE - *Write your exercise goals, then chart your improvement each time you workout. Reward hard work with a special treat after reaching your target, (e.g. new sporting equipment, piece of jewelry, non-fat frozen yogurt sundae with fresh fruit and nuts, movie or concert tickets).*

FEEL BETTER KNOWING
YOU DON'T FEEL A DANGER SIGN

Among American women, breast cancer is the third-leading cause of death, (following heart disease and lung cancer). Yet breast cancer is nearly 100 percent curable when the tumor is detected early and hasn't spread. For this reason, monthly breast self-exams (BSE) are essential for women over 18 years.

Lie on your back and, pressing firmly, move your three middle fingers up and down the entire breast in even rows. Do BSE at the end of your menstrual cycle and allow at least two minutes per breast.

EXTENDED CHALLENGE - *Most women's breast tissue has some lumpiness due to cysts. If you discover a small lump, hard knot, or thickening which doesn't feel normal, see your health care professional immediately and have it checked, just to be safe. Call 1-800-4-CANCER for cancer prevention and treatment information.*

GET ENOUGH SLEEP,
BUT NOT TOO MUCH

Too much sleep may make people soft, tired, and restless at bedtime. One study shows that long sleepers, (over 10 hours a night) have between a 1 1/2 and 2 times higher death rate due to heart disease, cancer, and suicide.

If you sleep more but feel less rested, make a change. For instance, try a new pillow, exercise more vigorously during the day, take a hot bath before retiring, cuddle your teddy bear, or sleep in a cooler room.

EXTENDED CHALLENGE - *Don't lose sleep over an occasional sleepless night, or one which extends well beyond the norm. See a doctor to check out possible medical or psychiatric causes if the problem persists for more than three weeks.*

WHEN SOMETHING ISN'T QUITE RIGHT, SEE A DOCTOR

Medical self-care starts by being aware of unusual conditions and seeing a doctor with the following symptoms:

Unexplained lumps or swelling, changes in a mole, easy bruising, chronic coughing, persistent sores, severe depression, convulsions, bleeding gums, irregular menstrual changes, persistent sore throat or trouble swallowing, unexplained persistent itching, persistent digestion problems.

Also see your doctor with: Chest pain that radiates to the neck, shoulder, or arm; frequent or painful urination; loss of motor function, numbness; dramatic weight loss or gain; headaches with blurred vision or nausea; coughing or vomiting blood; rectal bleeding or blood in the stool; persistent thirst; recurring chills, sweating, or fever; prolonged insomnia or fatigue; unrelieved constipation or diarrhea; chest pressure or shortness of breath; abdominal pain 2 to 3 hours after meals.

Use common sense; visit with a doctor about these or other symptoms which seem to require diagnosis and treatment.

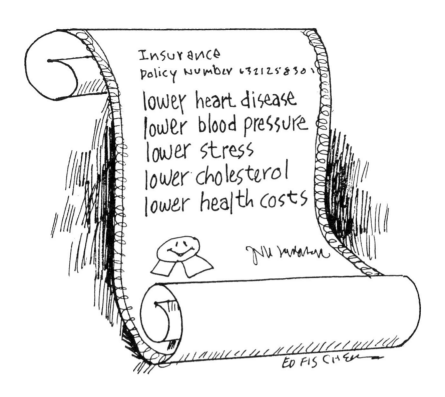

BEING FIT IS HAPPY INSURANCE

The bottom line of being fit is lower health costs! You pay fewer medical bills, and eventually lower your cost of health insurance. Exercise can help prevent obesity, high blood pressure, back injuries, stress-borne illnesses, and other costly medical conditions.

As you exercise, think of your arms and legs as "doctors" working to keep you healthy. Manage your fitness by using a lot of pull with these doctors. Go ahead, push your weight around!

EXTENDED CHALLENGE - *Spend the money you save on health costs on a piece of exercise equipment, athletic gear, or membership in a health club. Congratulations for earning the premium you've placed on fitness!*

HEALTHY BACK CARE

Back pain is the most common affliction known to man. Eighty percent of all adults have winced from stretched, strained, or torn back muscles and degenerative disk disease. Use the ideas in this chapter to help save back attacks.

ED FISCHER

Good posture helps prevent muscle tension, fatigue, stiffness, backache, and neckache. Disc and ligament damage can also be avoided with good posture. **Note**: To put less strain on your back, rest one foot higher than the other while standing.

Throughout the day, check you posture while standing. Lift your head far away from your toes with the chin tucked in. Tighten the muscles of your buttocks, letting your pelvis tilt forward.

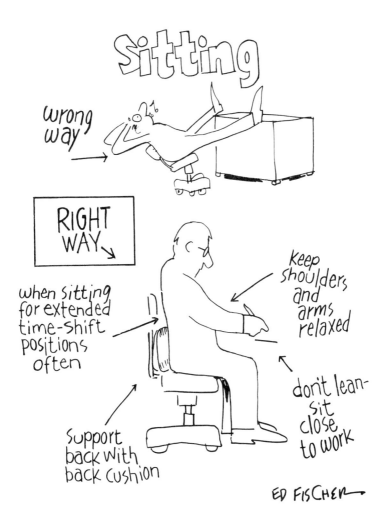

Sitting is harder on your back than standing. Use the ideas above to avoid back, shoulder, and neck strain. Don't sit still; stretch, shift, and wiggle your weight often. **Note:** Sitting cross-legged nearly doubles the stress on your spine and tissues.

Avoid sitting for more than an hour at a time without getting up and walking; get a drink, go to the restroom, or sharpen your pencil. Arrange your office so that you have to stand often to get things.

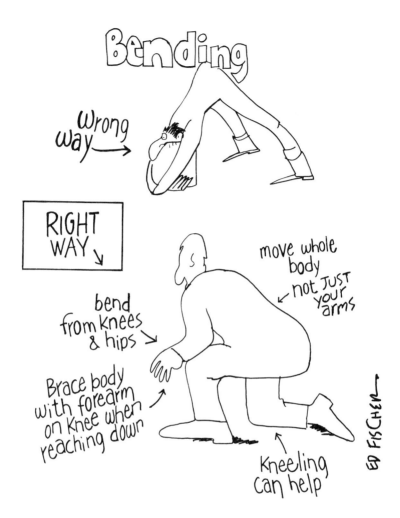

Safe bending reduces your risk of back injury and pain. Regular back exercises at least three times a week will do the same. Check with your exercise therapist or doctor before starting new exercises that strengthen and increase the mobility of a weakened back.

Never bend forward to pick up anything, even a paper clip, unless you support your weight as shown above, or brace yourself with a table or chair. Use your head, save your back!

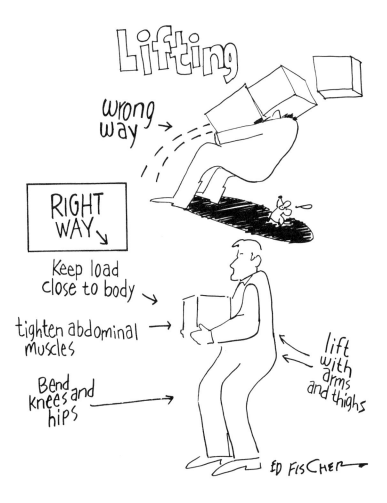

Improper lifting leads to the majority of chronic back problems. Ask someone to lift objects for you if your back is prone to injury. When possible, carry hefty objects behind you with extended arms. Also, avoid being overweight, a bulging belly begs for back pain!

Let your legs do the lifting; squat close to the load, bend your knees with your back vertical, grasp the object close to your body, then slowly stand up letting your legs do the work.

Pushing and pulling heavy objects can be as rough on your back as lifting! You can push twice as much as you can pull without straining your back. One major cause of back injury is loss of elasticity and strength of the back and abdominal muscles which support the back.

Stretch and strengthen weak and tense back and abdominal muscles everyday. YMCA, health club, hospital, or community education may offer fitness sessions for the back; or check the library for exercises you can perform.

Repetitive motions

wrong way →

RIGHT WAY ↘

keep loads small →

turn whole body- don't twist

lift with arms and legs

get close to load

tighten stomach muscles

ED FISCHER

Change position

Twisting is out; turning the whole body is in! Maintain back strength with correct body movements and daily exercises, even when your back is healthy and pain-free. Use slow, easy movements and avoid jerking. Back care exercise books suggest many helpful exercises.

WELLNESS QUEST ™

While sitting at your desk, exercise your back with... the slow head roll, chin to chest hug, knee kiss, buttocks squeeze, belly button to backbone press, straight-arm finger interlaced upward, and sideward stretches.

PLAY IT
SAFE

Take small steps to prevent accidents, injuries, and other pitfalls which account for great suffering and loss of life. Use self-care and safety methods to save your health and pocketbook too.

ED FISCHER

BE WARY OF MIRACLE CURES

Fake health products and services prey on people's desires to be happy and healthy the "easy" way. Be wary of diet plans, devices, drugs, health foods, cosmetics and treatments guaranteed to beautify or cure you. Read labels and study ads carefully; be alert to quackery.

 □

As a consumer, think long and hard before buying health products which make high-sounding claims. Ask your librarian for consumer product safety information, or call the consumer hotline, 1-800-638-2772.

EXTENDED CHALLENGE - *Analyze TV commercials, magazine ads, and billboards. Notice the fantasy each creates (e.g. success, intimacy, family, youth, or vitality claims). Such illusions appeal to subconscious desires to buy the product. By seeing through these dreams, you empower yourself to buy the product on merit.*

□

ED FISCHER

IS YOUR BLOOD PRESSURE
A TIME BOMB?

High blood pressure (called hypertension) is a quiet disease which can seriously damage the blood vessels and organs they serve; like the heart, brain, eyes, and kidneys. The first step in managing your blood pressure is having it measured once or more each year.

Have your blood pressure checked; it may signal the need for simple lifestyle changes, or medication. Free tests are often available at your drug store; better yet, purchase a home blood pressure kit.

EXTENDED CHALLENGE - *Lower blood pressure extends life. If after several tests your average score is borderline or high, follow the advice of your health care professional.*

ED FISCHER

ARE YOUR MEDICINES
OUT OF DATE?

Old medicines such as ointments, pain relievers, eye drops, and antibiotics break down over time and lose their strength or worse, form new chemicals which can be harmful. It is especially important to throw away old medications before they cause harm.

Check the expiration dates on all of your medications. Flush old medications down the toilet and rinse the containers before tossing them in the trash.

EXTENDED CHALLENGE - *Keep the poison control center's phone number posted near the telephone. Have a small bottle of syrup of ipecac handy in case the poison control center or hospital tells you to induce vomiting.*

CAUTION: if you notice green spots and a change in your voice, don't use

RIP OFF
RIP OFF

ED FISCHER

Read the label twice before taking medicine -- first when you pick up the bottle, and again before taking it. Avoid medical problems by taking the correct medicine and dosage at the times directed.

WELLNESS
QUEST™

Follow the "double read" method described on this page before taking any medicine, anytime. Teach this safety method to children by reading all directions aloud.

EXTENDED CHALLENGE - *Consider the medications you use for temporary, self-limiting conditions, (e.g. constipation, gas, heartburn, indigestion, colds, headaches, cramps, tension, muscle pain). Are medicines really necessary? Or are you able to ease the symptoms naturally through nutrition, massage, relaxation, exercise, humor - or just plain healing time?*

LEARN HOW TO DO CPR PROPERLY

CPR, (cardiopulmonary resuscitation) is vital for saving the lives of victims who suffer heart and breathing stopage due to heart attack, choking, electrical shock, drowning, or accident. Short courses are offered to teach these vital lifesaving skills.

Call your local Red Cross, hospital, continuing education office, or the Heart Association today and inquire about the next CPR course. Then sign up, and learn the simple methods which take only a few hours to learn, yet can save a life.

EXTENDED CHALLENGE - *Join an voluntary organization whose mission it is to help people during emergencies, (e.g. Civil Air Patrol, Red Cross, Salvation Army, police or fire reserves, local search and rescue teams). Call various organizations and inquire about helping out. You'll meet exceptional people.*

CANCER RECIPE
Fry in the sun

Planning to engage in outdoor fun?
Avoid the sizzling midday sun!
If you enjoy the "sunning" routine,
protect your skin with ample sunscreen (#15).

WELLNESS QUEST™

When exposed to the sun, avoid the most intense sunlight from 11 a.m. until 3 p.m., wear a hat, long-sleeve shirt, and SPF #15 or #20 sunscreen protection. As the ozone layer thins, the threat of skin cancer is very real.

EXTENDED CHALLENGE - *Plan your yard work and recreational activities for early morning or late afternoon; stay indoors or well-protected from the intense sun during midday.*

In certain emergencies, quick action is needed to save the victim's life. Calling 911 for medical assistance may take too long. For this reason, it's essential to know CPR and other first aid techniques designed to give immediate lifesaving assistance.

Call your school district or the American Red Cross today and inquire about first aid training courses in your area - then sign up! You'll be surprised how easy and enjoyable the procedures are to learn.

EXTENDED CHALLENGE - *Take a first aid course. Encourage a family member or friend to join you. Who knows, one day you may be the victim needing their help.*

The Heimlich, not the "hind kick" maneuver, saves choking victims. Use the technique if the person can't talk or breath, turns blue, and perhaps falls unconscious. The method described below can be applied to a standing or sitting victim. Prompt action can save their life!

Get behind the choking victim, place your fist with thumbside against their belly and below their rib cage. Place your opposite hand over the fist, then use both hands to force the food out by thrusting inward.

EXTENDED CHALLENGE - *Prevent choking by eating slowly, cutting food into small pieces, and not laughing or talking with your mouth full. Children need to be taught not to run around while eating - candy included.*

ED FISCHER

SAVE LIVES (AND TREES)
WEAR SEAT BELTS

Give yourself an "over-the-lap-snap" by securing your seat belt whenever in a car. Remember, most car accidents and injuries happen close to home. "Seat belt burns" are better than a busted and bloody windshield, (even at 25 mph). Slow speeds kill just as fast!

Fasten your seat belt whenever in a car. Insist that others do the same, especially in the city where most accidents happen! Seat belts also need to be used in cars equipped with air bags.

EXTENDED CHALLENGE - *When you drive, refuse to start the engine until each passenger has fastened their seat belt. For fun, see who can snap it on first after the last door closes.*

WASH HANDS
OR EAT GERMS

Cold and flu viruses are passed along via the hands. To prevent this from happening, wash your hands before handling food, keep your hands away from your mouth and nose, and avoid sharing the same piece of food, expecially during the cold and flu season.

Before handling food, rinse your hands under warm soapy water for 30 seconds to wash away germs and viruses that might be on them. Don't give disgusting germs a helping hand into your body!

EXTENDED CHALLENGE - *Take extra precaution. Insist that family members wash their hands before preparing food at home. Wash eating plates and utensils with plenty of hot, soapy water, especially during the cold and flu season.*

REMOVE TARTAR (NOT TEETH)
WITH PROPER FLOSSING

Enamor your enamel with brushing and flossing. Flossing once a day or even once a week will help remove the sticky tartar that builds up daily. This smart action helps prevent gum disease and tooth decay, sweetens the breath and brightens the smile!

Make brushing teeth after breakfast and before bedtime a daily habit. Include flossing as a chic part of your high fashion routine. You'll be stylish, trendy, and in the groove!

EXTENDED CHALLENGE - *To help make flossing part of your daily routine, have the floss within arm's reach at designated times, (e.g. after shaving, removing your contact lenses, on the toilet, or in the shower). Rinse your mouth with water or mouthwash after you've flossed to remove all debris.*

REGULAR TRIPS TO THE DENTIST CAN SAVE ADVENTURES WITH DENTURES

If wisdom teeth could speak, they'd tell you the tooth truth: A routine cleaning and checkup every six months will help keep plaque and tartar buildup under control. Decay, abscesses, swollen red gums that bleed easily, loose and impacted teeth will need to be treated.

If you haven't seen your dentist for a year, schedule a dental exam today. Young children need checkups too! Help prevent cavities by using a fluoride and tartar-control toothpaste and mouthwash.

EXTENDED CHALLENGE - *Protect your teeth from damage by not chewing ice, pens, or pencils. Wear a mouth guard during sports. Avoid sugar-sweetened gum and beverages. Eat sticky, chewy foods, starchy foods, and other foods high in sugars with meals, and not before bedtime.*

Hear! Hear! Next time you have a loud blast with music, turn it down. Remember, repeated loud noises can damage the delicate structures within the ear and cause hearing loss that worsens with age. Be especially careful of booming walkmans and blasting speakers.

What two sources of loud noises are you repeatedly exposed to? Take action to avoid them, wear ear plugs, or lower the volume. Share this sound health concern with your friends.

EXTENDED CHALLENGE - *Use ear plugs while mowing your lawn or using other small, noisy engines. Use ear plugs while playing with a rock band, or attending a loud concert.*

PUT ALL POISONS
UP AND AWAY FROM CHILDREN

Keep toxins away from toddlers. Store all soaps, cleaning supplies, medicines, oils, gasoline, cosmetics, insecticides, and other harsh chemicals out of the reach of small, unknowing hands.

If you live with a child or have children visit your home, lock up all harmful chemicals or put them out of reach. For extra safety, put on "yucky" stickers or draw the "yucky" face on all chemical containers.

EXTENDED CHALLENGE - *Double-check to make sure all harmful chemicals and tools in your garage are out of children's reach.*

Heavy decisions: Whether to be sexually active, and if so, how to avoid unwanted pregnancy and a variety of sexually transmitted diseases including gonorrhea, syphilis, chlamydia, herpes, and AIDS. All of these diseases can occur with the first encounter.

Before discussing and deciding sexual matters, consider your beliefs. Learn all of the facts, then weigh the pros and cons. Realize the serious, sometimes fatal results which can occur, even with first encounters!

EXTENDED CHALLENGE - *Write down 5 things you plan to accomplish during the next 5 years; then consider how an unwanted pregnancy or sexually transmitted disease would affect your goals. Realize that abstinence is the only guaranteed way to prevent STDs and pregnancy.*

ED FISCHER

Don't let a pregnancy catch you by surprise!   Discuss and plan the "best" time to have a baby so that you can comfortably handle the work and costs of parenthood.

Answer these questions: When is the best time for you to have (or father) a baby? Give three solid reasons to support your answer. What responsible actions will you need to take? Discuss your answers with your partner.

EXTENDED CHALLENGE - *Free information and counseling is offered by County Health Departments and various other organizations within most communities. Refer to Pregnancy Counseling in the yellow pages; then call for information and do some serious soul-searching before becoming sexually active.*

WILLIE FOUND OUT TOO LATE,
SOME THINGS CAN BE DANGEROUS!

Before launching into something new, carefully consider the possible outcomes, especially if things can backfire. If the venture seems well-grounded, go ahead and shoot for the stars!

Identify one thing that you currently do which could result in injury. What safety practices are you using to protect yourself? Resolve today to take extra precaution.

EXTENDED CHALLENGE - *Become a self-appointed safety committee at home, work, or school. Attempt to identify unsafe practices and conditions; then take corrective steps to eliminate the risks.*

YOUR CAR GETS A 5,000 MILE CHECKUP, MAYBE YOU SHOULD TOO

Routine medical checkups may spot physical disorders before organ disease has occurred. Changes in diet and lifestyle habits may then correct the problem before illness develops.

Call your doctor, health department, or worksite health service and find out whether it's time to schedule a checkup as part of your body care program. If so, make an appointment and keep it.

EXTENDED CHALLENGE - *Refer to the next page for ideas about when routine health exams and screenings are recommended. Remember that your individual health needs may require additional attention.*

HEALTH EXAM RECOMMENDATIONS

★ How often should you have a routine medical exam? The answer varies depending on whom you ask.

★ The main goal of periodic medical exams is to diagnose treatable diseases which have no symptoms in the early stages, (e.g diabetes, high blood pressure, some forms of cancer). Many conditions can be cured, or at least controlled if they are found early. For this reason, routine medical exams are recommended for healthy people who experience no symptoms of illness.

★ The interval between exams depends on your age. Every 5 or 6 years seems appropriate for people under 30 years. After 30 years a general health exam can be done every 3 to 5 years until age 40 or so. Between 40 to 60 years some recommend exams every 2 to 3 years, then annually after 60 years. Other authorities recommend a longer interval between checkups. Ask your physician and health insurance representative for their ideas.

★ The physical exam includes exams for thyroid, testicle, prostate, ovarian, lymph node, and skin cancer.

★ Pap smears for women need to be done for two consecutive years to get a baseline reading, then every year, especially for women with high risk. Pap smears and pelvic examinations are now recommended at age 18, or sooner if the girl is having sexual relations.

★ Women younger than 40 years probably do not need mammography unless a problem develops, or a family history of breast cancer exists. A baseline mammogram for breast cancer should be done between ages 40 and 49 years to determine what's normal for you, then yearly after 50.

★ Men and women 50 and older are encouraged to have yearly tests for colon cancer, including digital rectal exams and stool tests. After age 50, a sigmoidoscopy exam of the lower colon are recommended every three to five years.

★ Blood test for cholesterol, triglycerides, and blood lipids can be done every 5 years, annually if they are needed. A preteen baseline test is recommended for those with a family history of atherosclerosis. Blood pressure exams need to be done yearly, more often if there's a problem.

★ Tests for hearing and visual acuity should be done only if needed. Glaucoma screening, chest X-ray, and resting electrocardiography at age 40 and repeated as recommended by your physician.

★ As part of checkups, immunizations for diphtheria/tetanus (needed every ten years), flu shots (annually after age 65) and pneumonia (once after age 65).

★ Self-exams for skin cancer need to be performed monthly. Men need to perform monthly self-exams of the testicles starting during the teenage years. Women of childbearing age or older should exam their breasts monthly.

★ Testing should be done more frequently for people with specific health problems and increased risk factors. The best idea is to discuss the frequency of medical exams with your personal physician or health benefits representative.

EXAMINE YOURSELF

Heart disease, cancer and other diseases can be treated best when seen early. Between regular medical checkups, get into the habit of searching your body for unusual lumps, pain, coughs, discharges, scaly patches and other unusual symptoms.

Spend time today examining your body. Obtain from your library, or purchase a Home Medical Guide to instruct you. Seek medical advice if you detect anything out of the ordinary.

EXTENDED CHALLENGE - *For ways to conduct Home Physical Exams, obtain a <u>Healthwise Handbook</u> from Healthwise, Inc. P.O. Box 1989, Boise, Idaho 83701, (208-345-1161). The book also includes specific self-care recommendations for home treatment of over 130 of the most common medical problems. ($13.40 by mail)*

FACE LIFE
SQUARELY

Boldly look at each problem facing you. Greet each crisis as an opportunity to learn new skills and grow. Roll up your sleeves, dig in your heels, and work to solve problems in a forthright way.

ED FISCHER

MEET LIFE'S STRUGGLES HEAD-ON!

Life is one struggle after another. It's easy to turn one's back and blame others for all of the hard knocks. The challenge is to face each situation honestly by asking the right questions. In this way, the doors of opportunity are wide open!

Answer these questions to handle most problems: What part did I play to get myself in this situation? What can I do to correct this problem? How can I grow from this experience?

EXTENDED CHALLENGE - *Make a firm commitment to correct problems without banging heads. Greet the situation as a chance to grow, instead of growl. See the people involved, not as opponents, but as providers of a learning opportunity.*

Honest mistakes provide valuable feedback needed to solve problems and decide new directions. Learning from mistakes is vital for people on the grow. Next time you make an honest mistake, use it for your betterment and everyone's good fortune!

Think of a recent mistake you've made. Consider three ways you're wiser since that incident. Reflect upon one key way you've grown from the experience.

EXTENDED CHALLENGE - *Help others grow from your mistakes - share your experience and insights with a friend or family member. Good growing!*

Yes, pain is real! Some causes include hunger, abusive behavior, depression, stress, caffeine, alcohol, nicotine, food additives, aging, loss, injury, illness, disease, lack of exercise, and sleeping or eating problems. The first step to managing pain is finding the source.

When you're in pain, learn which methods of pain relief are best for your condition. Some techniques include relaxation, exercise, sleep, laughter, counseling, medication, and applying heat, cold or pressure.

EXTENDED CHALLENGE - *Ask your librarian for articles and books on pain management; then practice various techniques and learn how to resolve pain naturally. Consult with your health care professional or pain clinic if your pain persists.*

Go ahead and worry... if it helps you sort things out and propels you in the right direction. Worry is senseless when it prevents you from moving forward and getting on with life. From now on, use worry to drive you ahead; let go if it just spins your wheels.

Use worry to spark a positive action plan. Decide what healthy thing you can do to manage the worrisome event, or prevent it from occurring. Take action and achieve the desired results.

EXTENDED CHALLENGE - *Bounce ideas off a friend and arrive at the healthiest way to either change a worrisome situation, or ease your mind over it.*

IT'S HARD TO IGNORE PROBLEMS
YOU'VE SWEPT UNDER THE RUG

Don't keep your troubles under wraps. Face each problem and find thoughtful solutions. Life is much smoother when problems are exposed and straightened out. If left unattended, problems pile up and become stumbling blocks to happiness.

 □

Write down one problem you own. List all the possible solutions; let your imagination soar! Finally, weigh the healthy benefits and risks for each solution, pick the best one, and use it to solve the problem.

EXTENDED CHALLENGE - *If your solution doesn't work, go back to the drawing board; select, and use the next healthiest solution. Continue this process until the problem is solved.*

□

ED FISCHER

RATHER THAN CUSS YOUR PROBLEMS, DISCUSS THEM

When you're upset because your needs are not being met, talk with the person involved. Without judging or blaming them, tell the person exactly what happened, your feelings, and the effects upon you in terms of time, cost, self-esteem, or your relationship with them.

Use the ideas above to describe your problem, (e.g. I don't like it when you turn the channel when I'm watching a program. It upsets me when my show is interrupted. It lowers my self-esteem when I'm not being respected.)

EXTENDED CHALLENGE - *Besides getting your point across, listen to their side; then work to resolve the issue. If communication doesn't work, find a thoughtful friend or counselor who can help you figure out another responsible approach to take.*

ED FISCHER

NOBODY LIKES
A CONSTANT COMPLAINER

Do people shut you out, get defensive, or back away? Perhaps you're coming on too strong. Use factual "I messages" instead of blameful "you should" statements. "I messages" get your point across more effectively, preserve self-worth, and foster friendly feelings.

Use 4-part "I messages". Describe the situation factually, along with "I feel, I need, and I will.." (e.g. "I feel stressed when you give me this 3 page assignment. I'll be happy to finish the work, but I need more time.")

EXTENDED CHALLENGE - *Practice "I messages" at appropriate times when the other person is in an acceptable mood. If they're tired or busy, it's better to wait. Equally important is knowing when to switch gears and use "active listening" to connect with their needs. "I messages" alone without listening is sure to backfire.*

IF YOU'RE SAD, TELL SOMEONE

Feelings are made "good" or "bad" by how people choose to act on them. For example, crying and sharing sad feelings with a friend helps handle grief and is healthy. On the other hand, sadness which is avoided, or buried inside, creates stress and can become harmful.

Make all of your feelings "good" ones by acting on them in ways which help yourself and others. Avoid acting in destructive or hurtful ways. If necessary, call "time out" and gather your wits.

EXTENDED CHALLENGE - *Talk with a person trained in mental health if you're unsure how to handle your feelings, or if your emotions begin to control you.*

WHEN REACHING YOUR BOILING POINT, DON'T FLY OFF THE HANDLE

Feeling steamed? Cool off before expressing yourself! Count to ten, breathe deeply, smile inwardly and collect your thoughts.   Your "sizzle" will quickly "fizzle," and keep you out of hot water. After you've simmered down, express your displeasure in a relaxed, confident manner.

To master this skill, close your eyes and picture yourself staying cool in a heated situation. Breath deeply as you calmly rehearse what to say without vengeful anger. Practice will soon tame your jumpy responses.

EXTENDED CHALLENGE - *After training your nervous system with repeated visualizations, address the person in a composed way. Breath deeply and smile inwardly as you proceed. Feel terrific about keeping your cool.*

When life seems empty and useless, it is possible to work out the depressing feelings; they don't have to be permanent. It may be difficult and painful at first, but hope and well-being can be restored. Obtaining professional help is vital!

Seek professional help anytime you or a friend begins to feel worthless or hopeless. Comments like, "I wish I were dead," or "They're better off without me," are warning signs of desperation which need to be taken seriously.

EXTENDED CHALLENGE - *Waste no time! If feeling severely depressed or suicidal, call a pastor, counselor, helpline 1-800-333-4444, or 911 if help is urgently needed.*

BOUNCE BACK
FROM DISAPPOINTMENTS

Hang on! Sure you've messed up; and maybe you don't measure up to the big guys. Perhaps you've hit bottom with a series of hard knocks, but don't let that stop you. Be resilient! Realize it's not how far you fall, but how high you bounce back that counts.

Rebound from blunders with self-talk. Say to yourself, "Why feel blue when it's the best I could do? Besides, I know mistakes help me grow!" Then spring back with new plans for success and greater determination.

EXTENDED CHALLENGE - *Share your plans to improve a situation with a friend. By telling them your strategy, you make an informal commitment to follow through. Ask for their support and cheer.*

ED FISCHER

GET AWAY FROM PEOPLE
WHO INTEND TO HURT YOU

Take defensive action when people intend to harm you. First, get away from them! Ask others for help! Then seek advice about how to handle your feelings and avoid future problems. Talk to a pastor, teacher, counselor, social worker or law officer.

Identify one person you could turn to if you were a victim of someone's hurtful words or actions. Know that your safety and well-being is their concern.

EXTENDED CHALLENGE - *As a victim of physical and verbal abuse, refuse to feel guilty, ashamed, or vengeful. Seek counseling if you find yourself giving in to these feelings.*

ED FISCHER

HOME LIFE ISN'T ALWAYS
PICTURE PERFECT

At times, living is topsy-turvy. Excess stress, physical and mental illness, alcoholism, abuse, loss, and death can severely disrupt family functioning. Fortunately, people can learn to turn adverse situations around and bring themselves back to an even keel with appropriate actions.

If family life seems hopelessly confused and out of control, seek advice from a social worker or counselor. Use helpful suggestions which fit your situation to get yourself and family turned around.

EXTENDED CHALLENGE - *At least once a week, sit down as a family and discuss the new order. If that's not possible, engage a family counselor to foster discussions and offer ideas. In time, the family scene will be vastly improved.*

Balance "personal freedom" with a sense of "belonging," within your family. Allow others to be themselves, yet find ways to develop feelings of togetherness. Hold weekly family meetings to discuss both personal and family concerns, and to make plans for fun!

Conduct a family meeting; topics might include cooking, cleaning and T.V. viewing schedules, unfair family practices, what is most enjoyed about each other, a family goal, and one fun family outing for the week

EXTENDED CHALLENGE - *Select the most convenient day and time each week to hold family meetings - then make a commitment and do so. It may be helpful to take notes during each meeting, especially when family rules are being decided.*

LEARN TO COMPROMISE FAIRLY..

Don't have a falling out everytime you disagree. Look for ways to bridge the gap of misunderstanding. Listen carefully, talk calmly and move toward an agreement both of you can live with. A spirit of "give and take" can help move people closer together!

When you disagree, quietly sit down and discuss your needs; what exactly does each person want? Write each idea down along with the pros and cons. Finally, hammer out a solution which is fair to each person.

EXTENDED CHALLENGE - *While working your solution, make adjustments along the way until you and the other person find common ground.*

ED FISCHER

STAND UP FOR WHAT YOU BELIEVE, KNEEL FOR YOUR BELIEFS

Whether you stand, kneel, sit or lie down, seek to enliven your spirit. Hear the inner voice which comforts and heals. Nurture the spiritual part of yourself; discover the special meaning of life and the tingling ecstasy which is aroused.

Devote twenty minutes today seeking the source of wisdom, strength, and healing found within yourself. Find a quiet place and pray, meditate, or read inspirational ideas. Feel at peace with yourself.

EXTENDED CHALLENGE - *Each week, search for a different place where you can retreat and find tranquility; (e.g. chapel, park bench, riverside, garden, woods).*

Even if you possess superhuman powers and leap tall buildings in a single bound, there will be times you'll need assistance in coping with seemingly impossible situations. Fortunately, there are caring people positioned to help you overcome difficulties and get on with life.

Recognize those times you need group support. Be willing to feel the moment of indecision as you give up your foothold and surrender yourself to be helped. Brace yourself for the jolt and pleasure of upholding hands.

EXTENDED CHALLENGE - *Join a support group at church, school, work, or within the community when you are faced with an ordeal which seems overwhelming.*

ED FISCHER

Why carry a grudge? It wastes time and energy, and what does it accomplish? If someone causes you pain, find a healthy way to express your feelings, then move on. Remember, forgiveness is not forgetting what happened, it's giving up the revenge.

Forgive someone today for a past problem. Write your forgiving words, and reasons, down on paper, then reflect upon the ideas until they are taken to heart. This is your ticket to happiness!

EXTENDED CHALLENGE - *If you're not willing to forgive an injustice, decide what responsible action to take. It may be helpful to seek the advice of a thoughtful friend or counselor before taking action.*

ED FISCHER

TAKE TIME OUT

Lay back and loosen your shoelaces. Take a few minutes to gather your thoughts and restore your energy. At times, sitting on the sidelines can expand your view and improve your game plan; soon you'll be able to tackle your tasks with increased vigor!

WELLNESS QUEST™

Balance hard work with periods of relaxation at least three times today. For instance, take a brisk walk, whistle a happy tune, visualize your favorite place, visit with a friend, or just sit and enjoy the game

EXTENDED CHALLENGE - *Develop a weekly game plan designed to balance hard work and home responsibilities with periods of relaxation and fun; then execute your plan and feel like a wellness winner.*

COUNT YOUR BLESSINGS
INSTEAD OF SHEEP

Feeling discouraged because life seems nightmarish? Dream again! Your heart is beating, your lungs are breathing, and you have chosen to read this book. All is not lost! As you take steps to control your thoughts and dreams, high spirits will awaken!

Anytime you feel spent, revive yourself with a fresh spirit of thankfulness. Write 5 things for which you are most grateful. Reflect on the list before going to sleep, and upon waking each morning until you feel restored.

EXTENDED CHALLENGE - *Memorize your "thank list" and recall the ideas anytime you feel dissatisfied or restless.*

ED FISCHER

IN A RUT?
STRUT!

Feeling low? Stand tall, throw your head back, walk with snap and excite your body with lively activity. A vigorous body can revive the emotions and uplift the spirit in record time! From now on, bounce back with exercise and feel your spirits rise!

Take a peppy twenty minute walk today and think of each healthy blessing you have. Repeat to yourself, "Thanks for....." as you consider each gift life has loaned you, (e.g. fingers, rings, shoes, feet).

EXTENDED CHALLENGE - *Walk, think, and thank yourself out of ruts. Seek counseling if you're unable to hike to the high grounds of mental well-being after several weeks.*

ED FISCHER

DON'T JUST "HAVE" A NICE DAY-
"MAKE" A NICE DAY!

On gloomy days make your own sunshine! Don't depend on others to brighten your day. Studies show that "cheerful" thinking boosts the immune system and total health. Remember, the source of brightness shines from within!

Today when people say, "Have a nice day," respond by saying, "Thanks, and you make yourself the happiest day ever!" Then within 30 minutes, challenge yourself to find one wholesome way to sparkle.

EXTENDED CHALLENGE - *Take action to "make" each day special, especially if the sun isn't shining and things aren't going your way.*

SUPER ME

Take action to improve life by leaps and bounds. Empower yourself to reach personal heights of happiness and fulfillment. Follow the ideas in this chapter as you strive for excellence and seek your potential.

WEINER **WHINER** **WINNER**

ED FISCHER

PICK ONE

Choose the person you want to be: A "hot dog" who acts without thinking and often ends up in hot water; a "mad dog" who stirs angry feelings with ill-tempered thoughts; or a "top dog" who gains respect by using PMA (positive mental attitude) before acting.

Write down the key thoughts, feelings, and actions needed to become the type of person you seek to become. During the day check to see if you are thinking, feeling, and acting that way.

EXTENDED CHALLENGE - *Use repeated visualization to train yourself to become the person you desire. Each day, close your eyes and picture yourself acting, feeling and thinking the way you aspire. Soon your nervous system and self-image will be shaped to carry out your mission.*

SET MAJOR GOALS EACH DAY

As sole architect of your life, develop a daily blueprint, then follow your plans to shape solid results. For example, write down work to be done, phone calls to make, and free-time activities to enjoy. The lifestyle you design each day can build a highrise of wholesome success.

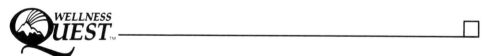

Think, better yet, write down one way to exercise your body, stimulate your mind, elevate your spirit, and get closer to people today. Carry out your plans and enjoy the positive results.

EXTENDED CHALLENGE - *At the end of the day, review your list and check off those tasks which were completed. Place unfinished items on the next day's agenda. Congratulations for being super organized!*

189

THINK MORE OF YOURSELF

No one can feel put down without their own permission. So why look down on yourself and dwell on your shortcomings? It's just as easy to reflect on life with optimism and create a positive self-image. Notice how self-worth expands when you affirm your strengths.

 _____ □

On your bedroom or bathroom mirror, tape small pieces of paper with positive "I am..." statements, (e.g. I am working hard. I am quitting tobacco. I am kind.) Recite these affirmations each time you look at yourself.

EXTENDED CHALLENGE - *Each day add 3 or more affirmations to the mirror for one month. Dig deep - search for qualities about yourself which are taken for granted. For an extra challenge, memorize the statements.*

□

COMPARE YOURSELF TO OTHERS

Go ahead! Compare yourself to a noteworthy person who has helped others! Feel inspired! Set lofty goals and extend your efforts so that one day you are the person others look up to! Remember, the tallest mountains are made from boulders and stones, so start small and build!

Each day write one task to complete on a piece of paper. At the end of the day, place this paper in a box if you completed your goal. In a short time, you'll be able to papier-mache a "victory" mountain!

EXTENDED CHALLENGE - *Read the biography of a person you admire. Notice the obstacles and struggles they overcame. Resolve to approach life with the same determination.*

THE VICTOR!

Start small! It's better than not starting at all! Merely place one foot in front of the other, repeat the action, and bingo, you've begun! Staying power will grow as you do more each day. The key is movement. Whether big, small, or microscopic... take steps and move!

Complete the following, "If I had one month to live, I would..." Write down your ideas. Be as wildly imaginative as you want. Then pick the activity which would be most fulfilling - and take steps leading that direction!

EXTENDED CHALLENGE - *Avoid saying "I can't"! Put your mind to the task and rise to the occasion. Saying, "Yes! I can!" will boost confidence and head you in the right direction. Small successes will soon lead to the winner's stand and generalize into other areas.*

ED FISCHER

BITE OFF MORE THAN YOU CAN CHEW

Don't be chicken! Sink your teeth into a new venture. Soon the discomfort of taking on another fresh challenge will stretch your appetite and expand your confidence and skill. Go ahead! Extend your love for life. Try something new!

WELLNESS QUEST™

Grow by taking on more. For example, learn to fix your bicycle, tune your car, bake a loaf of whole-grain bread, learn to sail, write a book, or join a club designed to expand your talents.

EXTENDED CHALLENGE - *With a family member or friend, take on a three-month challenge which can be accomplished together, (e.g. train for a marathon, build a canoe, remodel a room). Encourage each other along the way. Celebrate your growth at the end of your venture.*

TAKE A SHOT AT LIFE

Sail to new heights of personal achievement. Select one goal currently beyond your reach in the area of athletics, academics, job, or leisure time. Once your goal is defined, develop a course of action, and take off! You may feel uneasy in the initial stages of skill development, but soon your expanded confidence will have you soaring!

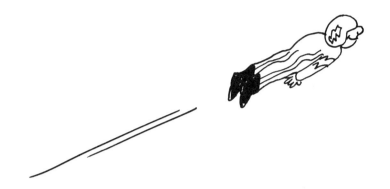

Live an inspired life. Discover your unique talents and special qualities, then display them by helping people! One day a monument may be built in your honor. You will have truly fulfilled your destiny. People and pigeons will love you!

Write the words you would want inscribed on your statue. Post the inscription by your bed. Before retiring, review the words and consider what actions you took during the day to achieve the standard.

EXTENDED CHALLENGE - *It's difficult to accomplish noteworthy goals alone. Find a person or group with similar aspirations and spend time with them each week developing your skills, (e.g. writers' group, Toastmasters for public speaking, computer club, swim team, theater group, chess league, investors' group).*

Hollywood and Madison Avenue create illusions that good looks, glamour, and youth expand self-worth. Such fantasies sell health and beauty products but tend to lower people's view of themselves as wrinkles, sun spots, sagging body parts, and other natural aspects of aging occur.

Pull the plug on the notion that one must be beautiful to feel worthwhile. Spend five minutes today considering your inner beauty. Identify at least three personal qualities which give a radiant glow to your life.

EXTENDED CHALLENGE - *Ask a family member or friend what quality they like most about you; then share your impressions of them. Repeat this experience with several people. It may seem awkward at first, however this activity can be fun and insightful!*

Replace the "dollar and cents" medical approach back to health with the "common sense" wellness practices suggested throughout this book. If illness or accidents do strike, empower yourself to heal from within using soothing music, relaxation, humor, and a zeal to heal.

If you're sick or injured, speed recovery. Visualize antibodies racing through your body, aggressively destroying invading germs. Picture healing enzymes flooding your body and restoring your health.

EXTENDED CHALLENGE - *Read the recent studies on the psychobiology of mind-body healing; then use the techniques to speed recovery. Dr. Bernie Siegel's books Love, Medicine and Miracles and Peace, Love and Healing are recommended. Find a doctor who believes in psychoneuroimmunology to encourage your "doctor within".*

LAUGHTER, BEST MEDICINE

Killer T-cells need a laugh too! Slaving day and night to stamp out invading germs and viruses can be pretty disgusting. A hardy laugh strengthens these tiny T-cell soldiers and boosts your line of defense against illness and disease.

For at least thirty minutes today, read, watch, or discuss something humorous and build up your immune system with lively laughter. It's free, it works, and it has no bad aftertaste!

EXTENDED CHALLENGE - *Find humor in the harmless blunders you make during the day. Laughing at oneself removes the sting when making mistakes.*

Call it medicine for the mind, emotional elixir, or body balm... studies show that wholehearted "fun" restores balance and promotes healing. Playing also helps mend fractured friendships. No wonder doctors and psychologists recommend daily doses of soothing, fun-loving play.

Treat yourself to a heap of fun today. Find a zany way to tickle your fancy. Go fly a kite, play checkers, build sand castles, or kick leaves. Lose yourself to the "kid" inside of you.

EXTENDED CHALLENGE - *Invite a family member, friend, co-worker, neighbor, or pet to play with you. Don't keep score; just play for the health of it and feast on the fun.*

IT'S HEALTHY TO SING HAPPY SONGS

Lift your spirit! Sing a cheerful song or play your musical instrument; be bold, allow others to hear it! Music provides rhythmic stimuli which dates back to the dawn of man. Music builds harmony between the body, mind, and spirit. Feel happy as a lark with musical spark!

While feeling frustrated with your work, caught in traffic, or bummed out, sing, hum, or whistle "Zip-a-dee-do-da" or other spirited songs, (e.g. "Theme from Rocky," "Impossible Dream"). Your heart will feel the joyful rhythm.

EXTENDED CHALLENGE - *Regardless of your age, learn to play a musical instrument; if you're an accomplished musician, teach another person the joys of playing. Music stimulates the logical and creative parts of the brain. It provides enjoyment and helps keep the mind lucid in later years.*

Start the day in the brightest way. Elevate your thinking with wholesome thoughts and the spirit of thankfulness. By looking forward to the day, you spark energy and perk your spirit!

WELLNESS
QUEST™

Before rolling out of bed, welcome the day by thinking of three enjoyable activities ahead. Consider what you can say or do during those times to make each experience even more special.

EXTENDED CHALLENGE - *At the end of the day, review your activities and give thanks. Promise to make tomorrow a special gift.*

MAKE A DATE WITH YOURSELF
TO HAVE FUN

Why be shy? Ask the key player in your life to go out and have a grand time. And don't turn yourself down! You deserve special treatment for all of your hard work! After your celebration, share the self-respect you felt with family and friends. They are part of the victory!

Spend at least 60 wholesome minutes today treating yourself to something special! Give yourself flowers, eat a favorite meal, go to a movie, or sing yourself a love song! Enjoy the special person you are with!

EXTENDED CHALLENGE - *Feel comfortable celebrating your successes alone. If you start feeling guilty about not including anyone, remind yourself that occasional times alone are important too - then enjoy! Your heightened spirit can be shared afterwards.*

HAVE AN AFFAIR WITH MOTHER NATURE

Escape artificial lights and sounds. Spending leisure moments strolling through a woods or garden can restore balance by uncluttering the mind and boosting the body's energy. Feeling close to nature brightens one's outlook and paves the way for a glorious day!

Weather permitting (or not), spend at least twenty minutes today walking outside and observing the beauty and tranquility of nature. Feel fully alive as you marvel at nature's glory!

EXTENDED CHALLENGE - *For the next month, schedule weekly treks into the wilderness. Visit the state and national parks in your region. Ask family members and friends to join your outings.*

CELEBRATE LIFE!

Celebrate life! Praise the people who have inspired you! Respect your body! Honor your mind! Exalt your spirit! Give thanks for your past good fortune and the bright future you are creating this very moment!

Spend at least ten minutes today celebrating life. For example, savor a sweet piece of fresh fruit while remembering two recent successes and giving thanks for each.

EXTENDED CHALLENGE - *Celebrate life! Plan a party for the sole purpose of sharing joy with family and friends. Let each guest know their presence makes your celebration of life very special.*

REACH
OUT!

Unleash your full potential. By helping others, you reinforce your value as a human being. Your pathway towards healthy living will cross the paths of many people. Helping them along the way will make your journey more glorious.

ED FISCHER

SMILES ARE CONTAGIOUS

When you meet a person who's not wearing a smile, give them one of yours. See how your grin grows on them. Think of how many lives you'll touch when they pass your smile along.

Pass your smile along to the people you face today, (unless you're riding the New York subway). See how many accept your invitation to be happy.

EXTENDED CHALLENGE - *Smile on people with charitable works - volunteer to cook one day a week at the homeless shelter; volunteer to be a big brother or sister for a disadvantaged youth; or find another kind way to help others smile.*

CALL AN OLD FRIEND

Bring back fond memories by writing or calling a friend and recalling a moment from times gone by. Remembering pleasant times together can brighten the day and rekindle fond feelings.

Write or call a distant friend today and recall a fun time you both shared in the past. Know that neither time nor distance can dim those treasured moments.

EXTENDED CHALLENGE - *Perhaps you've thought about it, now take action. Plan a reunion! Find the whereabouts of distant friends and call them before the week is over. Plan a time and place to get together and reminisce.*

Missed opportunities to visit with family are lost forever. However, it is possible to turn regrets into positive action. Take time from your busy schedule to talk with a family member; don't be in a hurry to finish.

Spend at least 20 minutes today talking with a family member. Realize that your experience will be logged in the heart forever.

EXTENDED CHALLENGE - *Make plans each week to carry out a meaningful conversation with a family member or relative. Find out what they're doing to stay well, (e.g. baking bread, reading a new novel, watching their favorite team, learning a new hobby). Share what's happening in your life.*

ED FISCHER

AVOID DRIFTING
FROM A CARING FAMILY

Most young adults pull away from their parents and seek independence. But how much distance is healthy? And when do self-serving interests create a point of no return? Only you can answer those questions and determine whether it's necessary to reconnect family ties.

Consider whether you're drifting away from family members. If so, decide what simple ways you can return to your roots. Take action, and enjoy the family bonds which slowly strengthen.

EXTENDED CHALLENGE - *Visit with family members once a week. If possible, join them for an enjoyable activity.*

BRIDGE THE GENERATION GAP
WITH ACTIVE LISTENING

We start from different places. Age, experience, and different points of view separate us. Yet, it's not necessary to grow apart. People can narrow the gap of misunderstanding through active listening. In small ways, there can be a meeting of the minds.

First, get your bearing; decide where you stand. Next, get in touch with the other person's needs through active listening. Finally, adjust your sights and agree on a mutual position which both of you can accept.

EXTENDED CHALLENGE - *Active listen when you're at odds with a person. Confirm with nods, paraphrasing, and reflective statements that you've heard them, (e.g. You're really upset because mom took your squirt gun.). Listening helps you check understanding and work through issues.*

Don't let words slip by. Avoid confusion and build closer friendships with active listening. From time to time, let people know you've heard what they've said with eye contact, nodding, and rewording their concerns, (e.g. "I sense you're really frustrated.").

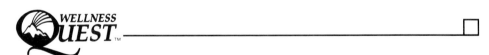

Spend at least five minutes "active listening" to a family member or friend today. Show in various ways that you are hearing them. Notice how the feeling tone improves as sensitivity is shown.

EXTENDED CHALLENGE - *Participate with family members or a close friend in a communication workshop, family enrichment program, or other human relations course designed to improve communication. Life has far fewer hassles when people understand each other.*

ED FISCHER

WILLIE THINKS
THIS IS A GUT LEVEL CONVERSATION

All true friendships are built upon emotional honesty. Revealing true feelings can earn trust between people. Over time a true sense of harmony and closeness develops, fostering physical and mental well-being.

Trust one person with honest feelings today. You will bring the most personal part of yourself closer to them. Go ahead, take a healthy risk, open up, and work to deepen your friendship!

EXTENDED CHALLENGE - *Cultivate a deeper friendship by regularly trusting a family member or friend with your feelings; take an equal interest in their feelings. Avoid judging or offering advice. Simply listen and show your respect for their feelings.*

SURPRISE SOMEONE WITH A SMALL GIFT

Produce grand feelings the good old-fashioned way with small acts of kindness. Give your friend a handcrafted gift, drawing, or poem. Show a friend you care by helping them without being asked.

Give a small gift to a special person today without expecting anything in return. Enjoy the moment.

EXTENDED CHALLENGE - *Make generosity a habit. At least once a week treat family, friends, schoolmates, and coworkers to small gifts, (e.g. fresh fruit plate, shared pitcher of herbal ice tea, help fixing or cleaning up, written compliments).*

ED FISCHER

TALKING UP TO KIDS
MAKES THEM FEEL TEN FEET TALL

Give children praise and watch them grow! Say specific things like, "You did a neat job mowing the lawn today, it looks great!" Expressing a sincere "good going" spurs "good growing!" Praise is the yeast which makes self-esteem rise!

At least three times today, give sincere and specific praise to a child or adolescent. Notice how their eyes brighten!

EXTENDED CHALLENGE - *Each day, recognize strengths vocally and often. Rather than nagging, pressuring, or showing disappointment when mistakes are made, tell the person how proud you are of their efforts. Encourage them to continue. Provide support if they ask for it.*

LEARN TO APPRECIATE
A COMPLIMENT

Many people find it difficult to accept a compliment. They tend to reject the good words by thinking, "I wasn't that good." It   takes conscious effort to soak up praise and feel terrific!

WELLNESS QUEST™

Fully appreciate each smile and friendly word sent your way today by thinking, "I deserve your praise, I am doing my best!" Return the compliment by saying, "Thanks, that's great to hear!"

EXTENDED CHALLENGE - *Studies show that people who believe they're liked, are more likable. People who think they're not liked act in unlikable ways. They make less eye contact, sit farther away, and reveal less information. The key to reaching out is first valuing oneself.*

Talk to a green plant! They'll absorb your words and carbon dioxide and give you oxygen in return. And plants won't judge you for venting anger and hostility. They offer a perfect way to aerate your blood, expand energy, and get things off your chest!

Each week, reward yourself or others with a green plant. Houseplants, especially the many types of philodendrons, can absorb indoor pollutants from the environment and make rooms warm and inviting.

EXTENDED CHALLENGE - *Plants remind us of life's natural rhythms; they are fascinating to be around. Make a commitment to fill living spaces with lush vegetation. Plant trees, flowers, and a garden outside. Regularly add potted plants indoors and enjoy their growing presence.*

HELP OTHERS

Reaching out to people improves the world; it might also boost your immune system. That's right, some research shows that people can help protect themselves from illness, overcome health problems, and even extend life with dosages of good deeds.

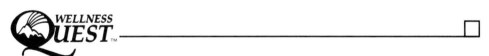

Without expecting thanks, be kindhearted three times today. Find ways to enrich peoples' lives with kind words and deeds. Give them cause to be happy! Give yourself reason to be healthy!

EXTENDED CHALLENGE - *Join or, if necessary, organize a group of caring people who are willing to serve others, (e.g. plant trees, care for elderly neighbors, tutor the poorly educated, register voters, coach Little League). Feel deep emotional bonds and fulfillment through volunteerism.*

SHARE SUPPER WITH SOMEONE SPECIAL

Reach out. Help the homeless, care for the sick, feed the hungry, and assist the disabled. Giving is beautiful when it is shared freely in the spirit of love, with no strings attached. Studies show that altruism lowers stress and raises self-esteem as goodness is shared freely.

Go out of your way to help less fortunate people. Give food, clothes, and money, but mostly your time and energy. Experience how charity gives rise to feelings of connectedness, the lifeblood of wellness.

EXTENDED CHALLENGE - *To obtain information about volunteer opportunities in your area, send a self-addressed, stamped envelope to VOLUNTEER - The National Center, 1111 N. 9th Street, Suite 500, Arlington, VA 22209, or call (703) 276-0542. Join a local group with goals that speak to your own.*

HUGS ARE HEALTHY-
AT THE RIGHT TIME

In studies, therapeutic touch has been shown to speed growth in premature infants, reduce headache pain, help bones knit, reduce swelling, raise hemoglobin levels, and enable hospital patients to sleep more comfortably. Loving, nonsexual touch also conveys warmth and affection.

If you're currently uncomfortable with embraces and other physical expressions of affection, use handshakes, pats on the back, and other casual ways to gain confidence touching people.

EXTENDED CHALLENGE - *Master the art of loving touch. At least a dozen times a day, hug the right people, pets, and stuffed animals. Feel your love flow with warm hugs and other intimate, nonsexual ways to touch family members and friends.*

MAKE EVERYDAY A NEW BEGINNING!

BOOKS FOR YOUR WELLNESS LIBRARY

Ardell, Donald B. Die Healthy Wellness Australia, 1989

Ardell, Donald B. History and Future of Wellness. Kendall Hunt, 1985.

Ardell, Donald B. High Level Wellness: An Alternative to Doctors, Drugs, and Disease. Ten Speed Press, 1986.(10 Year Anniversary Edition).

Ardell, Donald B. Wellness: The Body, Mind and Spirit. Kendall Hunt, 1989.

Ardell, Donald B. Planning for Wellness: A Pathway to Personal Excellence. Kendall Hunt, 1989.

Allen, Robert F. Lifegain. Appleton Century Crofts, 1981.

Bailey, Covert. Fit or Fat. Houghton-Mifflin, 1984.

Bailey, Covert. The Target Diet. Houghton-Mifflin, 1985.

Burns, David. Feeling Good. Signet Books, 1981.

Clark, Nancy. The Athlete's Kitchen. New England Sports Publication, PO Box 252, Boston, MA. 02113.

Cooper, Kenneth. The Aerobics Program for Total Well-Being. Bantam, 1982.

Cunning, Candy. The Eater's Guide. Prentice-Hall, 1983.

Davis, Marvel Harrison and Roache, Catharine Stewart. attrACTIVE WOMEN. Hermosa Publishers, 1988.

Hipp, Earl. Fighting Invisible Tigers: A Student Guide to Life in "The Jungle". Free Spirit Publishers, 1985.

Kemper, Don et.al. Pathways. Healthwise, Inc. 1985.

Powell, Don. A Year of Health Hints, Rodale Press, 1990

Schafer, Walt. Stress Management for Wellness. Holt, Rinehart and Winston, 1987.

Sheehan, George. Personal Best. Rodale Press, 1989.

Travis, John and Ryan, Regina. Wellness Workbook. Ten Speed Press, 1981.

ADDITIONAL RESOURCES

Wellness Quest offers a series of ready-to-use motivational wellness programs to any size organization. Programs are designed to inspire mass participation, boost morale, heighten wellness awareness, and build attitudes favorable to wellness through repeated validation.

The **QUICK QUEST PROGRAM** offers each participant a series of wellness challenge tickets to complete. People simply perform the challenge and qualify for prizes and awards. The Quick Quest program grabs attention and sparks interest in wellness by quickly leading people into action. People are regularly praised for their healthy accomplishments. Quick Quest is an enjoyable way to initiate a wellness program or rejuvenate an existing one.

The **CARE-CARD PROGRAM** brings health home! Each family is given a Health Care-toon book along with a series of weekly Care-cards to complete. Recognition and rewards are regularly given to pique interest and heighten involvement. The Care-card activity is an engaging way to reinforce healthy habits in the home.

The **FAMILY FUN AND FITNESS FESTIVALS** emphasize wellness as a family endeavor. Children and teenagers especially enjoy the novel health demonstrations and vibrant learning activities which emphasize self-worth. The festival contains spirited, stimulating, fun-filled trust-building activities and game show excitement.

WALK TALK TAPE FOR TOBACCO ESCAPE helps people replace the pleasures of nicotine with a highly spirited walking routine.

ENOUGH IS ENOUGH PUFF BUFF audio tape and program guide allows groups to participate in the "Non-smoker's Shuffle and make their own musical video.

BUCKET THEORY OF SELF-ESTEEM audio tape and program guide gets people singing, growing, and overflowing with feelings of self-worth.

HEALTH CARE-TOON SLIDE PROGRAM offers a complete program of Health Care-toons on slides along with a script which can be used in health presentations.

WELLNESS QUEST SEMINARS: Award winning professional speakers present seminars and training programs in vital health areas. Topics include Burnout to Balance, Unlocking the Winner in You, Building Superteams, Care for the Caregiver, Risk and Grow and more! Wellness Quest programs and keynote addresses are tailored to meet your specific group needs.

INDEX

ABOUT THE AUTHORS

Ed Fischer

Ed Fischer has worked as editorial cartoonist for three major newspapers and has daily cartoons distributed to over 60 newspapers in the United States. His work has appeared in Time, Newsweek, U.S. News and World Report, and in the World Book Encyclopedia. He has won many awards, including the Overseas Press Club award. Mr. Fischer has authored seven cartoon books including his latest What's So Funny About Getting Old? from CompCare Publishers.

Jeff Haebig, Ph.D.

Jeff Haebig has been a Health Educator for over 25 years. He is the founder and President of Wellness Quest, a company specializing in packaged, ready-to-use, organizational wellness incentive programs. He has produced a number of audio tapes including the Walking Tape For Tobacco Escape and the Puff Buff program in which people star in their own music video to discourage tobacco. Dr. Haebig conducts Family Fun and Fitness Festivals and presents workshops regionally and nationally.

YOUR CONTRIBUTION!

Submit a health cartoon and wellness challenge relating to physical, mental, social or spiritual well-being to Wellness Quest. If chosen, your contributions and name will be featured in the forthcoming Health Care-toon book. All ideas submitted become the property of Wellness Quest. Include a self-addressed return envelope if you want unused materials returned.

SEND YOUR IDEAS TO:

Wellness Quest,
1541 7 1/2 Avenue N.E.
Rochester, MN. 55906.

NOTES

ATTENTION

SCHOOLS, CHURCHES, BUSINESSES, HOSPITALS

Health Care-toon books are available at quantity discounts on bulk purchases for wellness incentives, fundraising or educational use.

For information write to:

Wellness Quest
1541 7 1/2 Avenue N.E.
Rochester, MN. 55906